Recognizing *God's* Timing for Your *Life*

THERE ARE MANY BOO[K] HOW TO HEAR THE VO[ICE] MUCH WRITTEN ON HO[W] PEOPLE FAIL NOT BEC[AUSE] GOD, BUT BECAUSE T[HEY] FOR THE FULFILLMENT OF GOD'S PROMISE. Know this, "There is an appointed time for everything. And there is a time for every event under heaven" (Ecclesiastes 3:1 NASV). This book will teach you how to discern God's timing based on the circumstances you face in your daily life.

Knowing *what* God wants you to do does not guarantee your success. Knowing *when* He wants you to do it guarantees your success. There is a purpose for what you are going through right now in your life. Maybe you are facing the loss of a job, or an unexpected trial. Life on earth happens in seasons. Nothing happens in our life without a purpose and a specific reason.

> Have you ever stepped out in faith to do something and failed and wondered why?

> Why do storms and trials come when you are in the midst of doing God's will?

> How does God communicate His timing?

> How do I know what I am supposed to be doing right now?

If you are looking for the answers to these vital questions, this book will help you find them.

ABRAHAM JOHN has been used by God internationally to proclaim the Gospel of the Kingdom. He is an ordained minister and is the founder and president of Maximum Impact Ministries which has trained more than 7,000 pastors and leaders in Asia and helped plant more than 80 churches. He is the author of other books including *Sin, Flesh and the Devil; Overcoming the Spirit of Poverty* and *Seven Kinds of Believers*. He is married to Tahnya and they live in Syracuse, New York with their three children; Rachel, Joshua and Renee.

MAXIMUM IMPACT
MINISTRIES

{ Maximum Impact Ministries
PO Box 3128
Syracuse, NY 13220
MAXIMPACT.ORG

There are few things in life that are more essential to personal success than timing. Most people become fixated on the "whats" of life; what school to attend, what career path to choose, what car to buy, what person to marry, what investments to make etc... Much of the time however, the deciding factor between success and failure is not what you choose as much when you choose to do it.

The Bible teaches us that God is the creator of both time and space and that He has designed a timing for "every purpose under heaven" (Ecc. 3). Because He is the author of time, He has promised that if we walk in His wisdom He will teach us how to redeem it.

In this compelling book Abraham John shares what he has discovered about the importance of spiritual timing in life and ministry. Using many examples from his own experience and the word of God, Abraham reveals many of the keys to identifying God's timing in your life and shows how you can reconnect with His purpose for your life if you have gotten out of sync with His plan. Recognizing God's Timing will impact your life with hope!

Pastor John Carter
Senior Pastor, Abundant Life Christian Center
Syracuse, New York

It is a timeless and much needed truth for the body of Christ, that which my friend Abraham John is addressing in this important new book.

Being a follower of Jesus Christ is not about holding a certain set of rules or tradition, it is about moving with and in the Spirit of God. Understanding the promptings of HIS Spirit, or as Pastor Abraham is putting it *Recognizing God's Timing For Your Life,* is the vital point to become or to be a true follower of Jesus.

It is a crucial thing for every single believer, for every church; to know, to understand, to get a revelation of God's visitation.

This book will help you to know and understand the visitation of God. While reading, the Holy Spirit will give you the revelation you need to recognize God's timing. So be ready for a life-changing encounter and a new and deep revelation of God's Timing.

Pastor Ivano Lai
Senior Pastor Swiss Pentecostal Assembly, Bern, Switzerland

Pastor Abraham has written a practical book for everyday Christians. His down to earth life experiences, as well as biblical illustrations lead the reader to understand how God moves in the seasons of our lives through painful experiences even more effectively than through the pleasant surprises. He says, 'Every new season comes with a new challenge and every new challenge comes with a new revelation of God.' Every Christian can grow by reading this book.

Pastor Frieda Maclear
Pastor of Missions Orchard Road Christian Center, Denver, Colorado

There is a divine timing in the release of this book. Abraham John has nailed it. With great spiritual insight he carefully lays out how God's plan for the world and for each of us is according to His timetable. Without a mature understanding of these principles we will live a life of ongoing frustration. I recommend *Recognizing God's Timing for Your Life* to anyone who is serious about moving in God's timing.

James Pielemeier
Founder and President
Legacies of Life Association, Tuscon, Arizona

God wants you to know about spiritual timing and how to discern your season. Pastor Abraham John clearly brought out the truth about God's timing in this book. He grounds his message in Biblical teaching, showing God's plan and His timings for our life. He lays scriptural foundation then gives practical advice as to how to apply these principles in our lives. His ministry has blessed me, and you too will grow in Christ as you read this book.

Rev. Dr. K. Jacob
Revival Christian Ministries, Trichy, India

"*Recognizing God's Timing for Your Life*" is at least as important for staying on God's ways for us as knowing and understanding who we are in Jesus Christ and what God's callings upon our lives are. The more I have reflected on what God gave to the heart of my dear friend Abraham when he was writing this book and the more I look back into my own life and into the lives of other Christians, the more I understand the importance of recognizing God's timing. I very much thank Abraham for allowing God to use him to share this important truth to other believers in Jesus Christ. May many Christians be blessed by the content of this book and walk successfully in the ways of God.

Juergen Lauber-Noell
Director of Maximum Impact Germany
Wetzlar, Germany

Recognizing *God's* Timing For Your *Life*

Discerning God's Timing and Purpose
Through Your Daily Circumstances

"Jesus answered, "At sunset you say we will have good weather, because the sky is red. And in the morning you say that it will be a rainy day, because the sky is dark and red. You see these signs in the sky and know what they mean. In the same way, you see the things that I am doing now, but you don't know their meaning." Matthew 16:2-3 (NCV)

"I have observed something else under the sun. The fastest runner doesn't always win the race, and the strongest warrior doesn't always win the battle. The wise sometimes go hungry, and the skillful are not necessarily wealthy. And those who are educated don't always lead successful lives. It is all decided by chance, by being in the right place at the right time." Ecclesiastes 9:11 (NLT)

RECOGNIZING GOD'S TIMING FOR YOUR LIFE

Discerning God's Timing and Purpose Through
Your Daily Circumstances

Published by

Abraham John
Maximum Impact Ministries
P.O. Box 3128
Syracuse, NY 13220
www.maximpact.org
email: mim@maximpact.org
(720) 560 4664

ISBN: 978-0-615-32209-4

Printed and published in the United States of America by Abraham John
Copyright © 2009 by Abraham John

Please direct your inquiries to mim@maximpact.org

To God Almighty for His Indescribable Gift.

*For the Spiritually Hungry, Who Want to Have
More of God in Their Life.*

Acknowledgements

This work would not have been completed if it was not for the valuable input from a few people whom God brought into my life.

My wife, Tahnya, and our three children; Rachel, Joshua, and Renee, whom God is using to make me the person He wants me to be.

My Pastor and mentor, John Carter, whom God used to touch my life with His unconditional love. Pastor, your spirit of excellence and character are truly exemplary. Your insight and wisdom were truly a blessing.

Nathaniel Bliss, who offered his valuable time and professional skills to edit this book. You are truly a gift from God. May the Lord reward you abundantly.

Andre Ivanchuk of Newline Creative, who designed the cover page and lay-out. Your patience and courage to face any challenge produced the quality of this work.

Thank you to all of the partners and friends of Maximum Impact Ministries for your prayers and support. You are true heroes of faith.

Contents

Preface

ARE YOU WONDERING ABOUT THE EVENTS THAT ARE HAPPENING IN YOUR LIFE, AROUND YOU AND AROUND THE WORLD? Are you not sure of what you are actually supposed to be doing right now? You hear about the signs of the end times on everyday news and you do not know what to expect next. The unsolved mystery and the struggle of the Middle East problem, brewing or brooding economic meltdown, and political uncertainty in almost every country in the world are concerns that are troubling people everywhere.

This book will help you to have an unshaken trust in God in a shaky world. This book will also teach you how to discern the times in the spirit based on your natural circumstances. God wants you to know for certain, what is happening to you and how you should move forward.

Most people live in the regrets of yesterday's decisions saying, "I wish I had only known ...," or, "I wish I had made a better choice" or even "I wish I had one more chance." I cannot imagine that there is a single human being on this earth who has not made one of those statements in their lifetime. I have said these many times in my life. Most of us gain wisdom either after the fact, or when we made the decision and suffered through the mess.

Is there a way we can know things ahead of time and make the right choices in life? Instead of being guided by past mistakes, is there a way to gain wisdom to guide future events? Is there a way to know the purpose of what is happening in your life so that you can make decisions with boldness? Yes, there is a way to know spiritual timing by discerning your immediate circumstances. In His wisdom, God provided a way for us to know and discern *what* is happening in our life and *why* it is happening.

God wants all of His children to live in His perfect will and the only way to do that is to know for sure what the perfect will of God is *before* we go through something. Many times we know the will of God concerning a matter after it has occurred.

As someone said, "To find the way to where you are going, the first thing to know is where you are right now." If you do not know where you are in life, you will not know how to go where you want to be. The same is true concerning what is going to happen in your future; you need to know what is happening in your life right now and why it is happening.

I was not raised with this kind of understanding. Growing up, I had no clue about my purpose, vision, or destiny. Nobody taught me about those things. My parents fed us, clothed us, sent us to school, and told us to pray and to go to church. Though they were spirit-filled believers they never talked to us about our purpose, call or spiritual timing.

When I was a little boy, one of my favorite stories was about a jungle boy who was raised by wild animals. When he became an adult, he came to a village but did not know how to relate to people or live like a human being. From the outside he looked like a human being but he did not know how to think or act as a human being.

I was like that jungle boy in many ways. I grew up without knowing how to cope with life, society, God or myself. I was taught that everything good on this earth was sinful and belongs to the devil; that God's people do not belong to this earth, they are pilgrims. The earth does not belong to us for we have nothing on this earth and there is nothing to enjoy in this life. Once you were saved and filled with the Holy Spirit, the next steps were to be miserable for the rest of your life and wait for the Second Coming or die and go to heaven.

Those were the slogans of the "theolugly" (that is a new word I made up for wrong theology pronounced theol-ugly) of the church I grew up in. They taught me that if I want God to love and accept me, I need to dress and behave in a certain way. I found out later that this thinking came from religious spirits that cause people to improperly interpret scriptures and use them to keep people in bondage through legalism.

I did not know there was a call of God on my life. I was kind of raised up by God just like the jungle boy was raised up by wild animals. The Holy Spirit began to teach me about life, purpose, destiny and God's timing on this earth. I could have avoided much pain if I had known better.

I found that God works in seasons and not according to our clock. The clock was an invention of man used to regulate events; not to show the real "time." What we call "time" is not "time" to God. He is outside of time because He lives in eternity. Everything happens in our life in a certain time or season. The Bible says,

> "To everything there is a season, a time for every purpose under heaven." (Ecclesiastes 3:1)

We guide our life and future by the decisions we make today. There are some decisions in life that have power to alter our destiny or change the course of our future. Choosing your career or your education are decisions made during certain seasons of life and it is very difficult to change them later.

There are decisions that cannot be reversed once you make them. Choosing your spouse (we live in a society that believes in divorce, but it never fixes the real problem), when to have children, your actions; these are made once and for all and cannot be reversed.

If one action can alter the course of our future, then we need to gain wisdom and understanding about God's timing for our lives so that we can lead our lives and be prepared when the time comes to make major decisions.

The Psalmist says in Psalm 90:12, "So teach us to number our days, that we may gain a heart of wisdom." Jesus said, "When the Holy Spirit comes, He will show us things to come." (John 16:13)

God does not want us to live looking back and worrying about unfinished tasks or trying to fix the past. He wants us to leave the past behind and press toward the future with boldness and great assurance.

From the Word of God and from my experience I have found how to recognize God's timing in my life. Anyone can identify God's timing in his life. You do not have to have a theological degree or read your Bible twenty-five times, even though they both are good for your life. God has made His plan and ways clear to us, but the natural man is not capable of understanding them (Psalm 92:5-6).

I believe this book will help you learn how to discern God's timing and season the next time it arrives and make decisions accordingly. I do not make any claim that the revelation contained in this book is exclusive regarding this particular subject. As the Bible says, "Now our knowledge is partial and incomplete." (1 Corinthians 13:9) (NLT) God bless you.

Author

Chapter 1

WHAT IS GOD'S TIMING?

"There is an appointed time for everything.

And there is a time for every event under heaven." Ecclesiastes 3:1 (NASB)

HAVE YOU EVER WONDERED ABOUT THE PURPOSE OF YOUR EX- ISTENCE? Whether or not you were born to do something signifi- cant? Does it seem like your life is going around in cycles? Does it seem like you are going from one problem to another and from one season of pain to another? Do you feel left out or that you missed your season?

Remember this, you are not an accident and what is happening in your life is not a surprise to God. You may have spent most of your life going through cycles but God was trying to get your attention. He was trying to communicate something very important to you. This book will help you to know how to get free from that and how to find God's hidden purpose in every circumstance in your life, especially when you feel 'stuck' on your spiritual journey.

Are you wondering what you are supposed to do with your life right now? Do you wish to know what God is up to next or why you are suddenly going through trials as never before? Are you at a turning point in your life and do not know which way to turn?

Do you feel like giving up and forgetting about every promise that God gave you? You might say that you have prayed and waited on God but no answer came. You may have cried all night until your tears dried up. In your heart, you may have questioned God's character and faithfulness. You might be asking why God is not fulfilling His promises that you have been believing for. Or, why God is not blessing you like He is blessing so and so. How come you never seem to have any breakthroughs in your life?

One thing you need to understand is that God is not moved by your kicking and screaming, your talent or education. He works according to His season and timing. Your success in life depends upon your ability to recognize God's timing and season for your life. You have a specific time in God's timetable and your season will come. If you missed one season cheer up, the next season will come.

This book was birthed as a result of my own experience of trying to figure out what God was doing in my life in different seasons. I started out in the ministry with a huge dream. I thought I was going to go out and win the world for Christ. Many times when I thought I was close to a breakthrough a sudden unexpected trial came instead. I did not always understand the purpose of those trials. So, I moaned and complained and finally God would rescue me. I went through that cycle repeatedly without knowing what was actually happening. There were other times I became discouraged and wanted to give up. Now when I look back I understand that many of those incidents that appeared to be trials were keys to my next breakthrough.

It was not always an easy road. I was caught off guard with challenges that caused enormous pain in my life. Some of those I could not believe that as a child of God I would have to go through, or that God would even allow me to go through them. Praise God that all things worked together for my good at the end (Romans 8:28).

However, if I had not gone through it all I would not have received this powerful revelation from God. The *test* you are going through right now in your life will be your *testimony* in the next season. The *pain* you overcome in this season will be the key to your *passion* in the next season. The *battles* you win in this season will be the platform for *promotion* to the next season. The problem you are facing right now may be the answer to prayer you have been asking for. God may send an answer to your prayers wrapped in a problem. When you look at the outside you see only the problem, but once you un-wrap it with God's wisdom and patience, you will see the divine purpose hidden in that problem.

In life, everything has to do with timing. In fact, our natural world functions according to times and seasons. We have years which are divided into four seasons and twelve months. A month is divided into weeks, a week is divided into seven days, and days are made of hours, minutes, and seconds. Everything you do on this earth is governed by hours and minutes. The spirit world is much more organized and runs according to specific times and seasons. All truths are parallel and it is our responsibility to learn to discern the time in the spirit. The Bible talks quite a bit about spiritual time and season.

Ecclesiastes 3:1 says,

> "To everything there is a season, and a time to every purpose under heaven."

Ecclesiastes 3:17 says,

> "...for there is a time there for every purpose and for every work."

Ecclesiastes 8:5 says that,

> "...a wise man's heart discerns both time and judgment."

Jesus talked frequently about spiritual timing. He often said the hour has come, or, the time has come. Below are some of the examples;

Jesus asked in Luke 12:56,

> "...how is it you do not discern this time?"

In Luke 19:44 Jesus laments that Jerusalem,

> "...did not know the time of your visitation."

> "But the hour is coming, and now is, when the true worshipers will worship the Father in spirit and truth..." (John 4:23)

> "...Are you still sleeping and resting? The time has come for the Son of Man to be handed over to sinful people." (Matthew 26:45) (NCV)

> "When I was with you daily in the temple, you did not try to seize Me. But this is your hour, and the power of darkness." (Luke 22:53)

His birth, ministry and death on the cross all had a particular timing. The Bible says Jesus was born in the fullness of time.

He performed miracles according to spiritual timing.

> "...Dear woman, why come to me? My time has not yet come." (John 2:4) (NCV)

He died and left the earth according to spiritual timing.

> "...The hour has come that the Son of Man should be glorified." (John 12:23)

> "Now before the Feast of the Passover, when Jesus knew that His hour had come that He should depart from this world to the Father, having loved His own who were in the world, He loved them to the end." (John 13:1)

In none of the above scriptures was Jesus talking about the Roman clock tower that was put up in Jerusalem. He was talking about the spiritual timing or the new season He was about to enter. In John 20:21, "Jesus said, "Peace to you! As the Father has sent Me, I also send you." If Jesus had to follow specific times and seasons for each and every thing He did and happened to Him on this earth, we need to follow the same example for our lives.

Spiritual timing is to know and discern what God is doing in your life *right now* and what He wants you to do at this particular season in your life: It is knowing where He wants you to be *right now* and learning to embrace and maximize it: To gain wisdom to discern what is happening in the spirit based on what you are experiencing in your natural circumstances, and make the right choices based on that discernment.

The Bible says,

> "I have observed something else under the sun. The fastest runner doesn't always win the race, and the strongest warrior doesn't always win the battle. The wise sometimes go hungry, and the skillful are not necessarily wealthy. And those who are educated don't always lead successful lives. It is all decided by chance, *by being in the right place at the right time.*" (Ecclesiastes 9:11) (NLT) (Italics added)

Jesus rebuked the Jewish leaders of His time because they failed to recognize God's timing for their lives. One of the reasons they did not receive the ministry of Jesus is because they did not know that the world had entered a new season by the coming of the Lord. They wanted to continue in the past season.

Jesus said in Luke 12:54-56,

> "...Whenever you see a cloud rising out of the west, immediately you say, 'A shower is coming'; and so it is. And when you see the south wind blow, you say, 'There will be hot weather'; and there is. Hypocrites! You can discern the face of the sky and of the earth, but how is it you do not discern *this time?*" (Italics added)

It is very clear from the above scripture that Jesus believed in different seasons in the spirit. He is giving us a key to discern God's timing based on the natural circumstances. If we notice the patterns of the sky we can predict the weather of that day. In the same way, if we notice the signs of what we are going through in our lives we can know the time and seasons in the spirit.

There is another incident where Jesus wept over Jerusalem because the people in the city failed to recognize their season of God's visitation. Luke 19:41-44 says,

> "Now as He drew near, He saw the city and wept over it, saying, "If you had known, even you, especially in *this your day*, the things that make for your peace! But now they are hidden from your eyes. For days will come upon you when your enemies will build an embankment around you, surround you and close you in on every side, and level you, and your children within you, to the ground; and they will not leave in you one stone upon another, because *you did not know the time of your visitation.*" (Italics added)

Jesus is not talking about the natural time. He is talking about the spiritual season they just missed because they did not know how to discern the spiritual time. The visitation of God they had been waiting for nearly 4,000 years had finally come and they missed it because they failed to recognize God's timing. The Messiah, whom the prophets had foretold and the entire Old Testament portrayed, came and lived among them but they did not receive Him because they did not know how to recognize the new season the world had entered.

KAIROS AND *CHRONOS* TIME

The Bible uses the words time(s) and season(s) 830 times collectively. There are two major words that are used in the Greek to describe time. One is *Kairos*, which means the natural time or the "right now time" in this earthly realm. The other one is *Chronos*, which means seasons, duration in which something occurs or chronology of events. *Chronos* is mostly used in relation to God's timing or seasons. *Kairos* is used in relation to our time or the opportune time. God works in seasons. He does not keep a 24-hour watch on His wrist like we do.

Discerning God's timing for our lives is so important that it can mean life or death. In Noah's day the people failed to recognize the season and they all perished. It was a time of great pain and God gave them an opportunity to escape the judgment, but they ignored it and perished in the flood. Jesus said in Matthew 24:36-39,

"But of that day and hour no one knows, not even the angels of heaven, but My Father only. But as the days of Noah were, so also will the coming of the Son of Man be. For as in the days before the flood, they were eating and drinking, marrying and giving in marriage, until the day that Noah entered the ark, and ***did not know until the flood came*** and took them all away, so also will the coming of the Son of Man be." (Italics added)

The above scripture talks about two different times. One is *kairos* and the other is *chronos*. Jesus said that no one knows the day or hour of His coming. That is talking about the *kairos* time or our natural time and day. Then, He is talking about the people in Noah's time, those who missed their spiritual timing. That talks about the *chronos* time. They did not know that the flood was coming until it actually arrived and it was too late.

When God moves out of the seasonal time (*Chronos*) and steps into a particular circumstance at a specific time (*Kairos*) on this earth, it is called a miracle or a breakthrough. Another example for *kairos* time is Psalm 102:13,

"You will come and have mercy on Jerusalem, because the time has now come to be kind to her; the right time has come." (NCV)

God works in our life in seasons. He wants you to be blessed and manifest His power and wisdom in your life. As I said in previous books, God had already prepared everything you need in your life before you were born. He brings it into your life according to His timing. The only problem we have on this earth is *ignorance*. One day I asked God to teach me about His timing. A year later He has revealed that to me and I am delighted to share it with you so that you will not miss the next season God has for your life.

The animal kingdom knows how to recognize time and seasons. They migrate and seek their food according to the change in nature. To be safe from the harshness of winter and to breed, some birds and animals travel hundreds of miles every year (Jeremiah 8:7). Some animals can sense the timing of natural disasters and they will move out of the area to a safe place before one occurs.

Many people fail not because they do not hear from God, but because they do not know when God is planning to fulfill that word. They step out and try to make happen what God has told them and they fail and blame Him for their failure. Just because you heard from God does not guarantee your success. What guarantees your success is when you know the exact time God is planning to fulfill that word.

I have found from the Word and personal experience that whenever God is getting ready to take you to a new season in your life certain patterns, signs and incidents happen that help us recognize His timing. We miss it most of the time because the events that happen are contrary to what we normally expect. Remember, God's ways are different than our ways.

When God speaks to you and gives you promises, there are some He is planning to fulfill immediately, some within a short period of time and others after many years. It is our job to know what He is planning to do and when He is planning to do it. When God gave the promise to Abraham about a son, He did not tell him that it would happen 25 years later. Neither did He tell Joseph about the timing of the fulfillment of his dreams. Jesus had to wait 30 years before He could begin the ministry God had sent Him to do on this earth. We are going to study in detail these saints and others; how they recognized God's timing and how some failed.

GOD'S PURPOSE, WILL AND TIMING

There is a difference between knowing God's purpose, His will, and His timing for your life. Purpose is the reason or the original intent for which He created you. God's will is knowing what to do to fulfill that purpose. And, His timing is knowing when to do what is required to accomplish it. For example, if God called you into business, that is your purpose. There are different types of businesses. Finding what type of business He wants you to do is knowing His will. When He wants you to do that business is knowing His timing.

This applies to any area of your life. If you know you are called to minister, that is your purpose. There are different types of gifts and callings of God. Knowing what type of ministry you are called to is knowing His will. Knowing where and when He wants you to minister is knowing His timing. God has a specific purpose, will and timing for every aspect of your life.

If time and seasons are that important to fulfilling our purpose on this earth, does God make any provision for us to recognize it? How do we know if our time has come? Though I cannot tell you *when* your time will come, I can tell you signs through which God communicates His timing. **There are seven different signs that I have found from the Word of God that He uses to communicate His timing to His people.** If we learn these signs we can recognize God's timing for our lives.

In the following pages I am going to explain them according to the grace that is given to me. God may use any of these in our lives as we enter into a new season. I believe this book will bless you to go to the next level in your life. The greatest prayer that I have for you is that God will help you through reading this book to recognize His timing.

Once again, God's timing is to know and discern what He is doing in your life *right now* and what He wants you to do at this particular season in your life: It is knowing where He wants you to be *right now* and learning to embrace and maximize it: To gain wisdom to discern what is happening in the spirit based on what you are experiencing in your natural circumstances, and make the right choices based on that discernment.

Chapter 2

NATURAL VS. SPIRITUAL SEASONS

"But solid food is for those who are grown up. They have practiced in order to know the difference between good and evil." Hebrews 5:14 (NCV)

WE NEED TO DISCOVER WHICH SPIRITUAL SEASON WE ARE IN BEFORE WE CAN KNOW GOD'S TIMING FOR OUR LIVES. Nature has four seasons; spring, summer, fall and winter. I believe human life has seven seasons; infancy, childhood, adolescence, adulthood, marriage, mid-life, and old age. Spiritual life also has seven seasons. When you are born again that is your spiritual infancy. Then, you enter into spiritual childhood and from there spiritual adolescence. Then, you move to spiritual adulthood and then to spiritual marriage, followed by spiritual mid-life, and finally, spiritual old age.

The spiritual seasons work in the same way as natural seasons. All truths are parallel. What I mean by that is to complete one season in the natural you go through different stages of growth. When you are a baby you start with wearing diapers and when you become a toddler you will start wearing "pull-ups." You start crawling and stand up with support.

To complete one spiritual season in your life you need to enter into smaller seasons in the spirit or go through different stages. The trees and plants go through different stages of growth. First the buds come, then the flowers, and finally, fruit.

In the natural season, to complete childhood you need to go from First Grade through Eighth Grade. When you go from one grade to another in school it is a big change. You might change schools or towns and the mode of how you get to school. You may also have different teachers.

To complete adolescence people usually complete high school and might go to college. Can you see that this is a big change? Or, it is like going from junior high school to high school. Each season is broken down into smaller pieces of change. Similar things will occur in the spirit. God will bring circumstances and people into your life and allow you to go through some difficult times.

Each season in life is very important and unique. The enemy also has an alternative plan for each of your seasons. He tries to attack you from the time you are born—and even sometimes before you are born. Childhood is very important because it forms your spiritual, social, and personal belief systems. It is the time of laying the foundation and if the foundation is weak or laid incorrectly, the entire structure can be weak. If the enemy can get you at that point he can alter your entire future and even destiny.

Sometimes he will use parents, relatives, abuse, teachers, religious leaders, friends, unusual incidents, or anyone who is influential in your life to cause defects in your spiritual and emotional formation. Regardless of what happened to you when you were a child, God can override the enemy's plan and bring healing and restoration for His purpose to come to pass in your life.

God expects each of His children to grow up spiritually. The Word of God is the food for our spirit. The more a baby Christian drinks the milk of the Word, the stronger his or her spirit becomes.

> "As newborn babes, *desire* the pure milk of the word, that you may grow thereby." (1 Peter 2:2) (Italics added)

We need to notice that the above scripture does not tell the newborn babies to eat or drink the milk of the Word, but only to desire the milk. The word used for desire in the Greek is '*epipotheo*' which means long for, to long after, pursue with love or to lust.

God knows and we know that a newborn babe cannot go to the store or to the refrigerator in the kitchen and get his milk. He can only *desire* to have milk. If the baby does, he will get the wrong thing and cause danger to himself. Someone needs to provide for or feed that baby.

It is also important that we watch what goes into a baby's mouth. A baby does not know what it should eat and what it should not. Everything the baby finds goes into its mouth and that can cause great danger to the baby.

Another thing about milk is that you drink it and not eat it. You do not need to chew the milk and it is interesting the Bible says that is the kind of spiritual food a new Christian needs to receive. I have seen many believers become born again and try to eat the *steak* of the Word. They do not want the milk; they look for the meat that is hard to chew.

They want to find out where Cain found his wife. Where did God come from? Who were the sons of God in Genesis 6? What was Paul's thorn in the flesh? There is no way they can digest these things even if their questions are answered. They will bring doubt and more questions.

When you grow up and become mature in the spirit, you will know in your spirit all the answers to the questions you have. The Holy Spirit will teach you everything you need to know because He is the Spirit of Truth.

How do you drink the milk of the Word since the Bible is not a liquid? In the natural the baby will cry for milk about once every three hours. When you get born again you need to feed your spirit by doing the following four things whenever you feel spiritually hungry for the Word.

You need to read your Bible regularly, think about w
speak it aloud to yourself as much as you can. Then, apf
circumstances whenever possible. That is the secret to sp.
you do not do these four things your growth in the spirit will be uc.
and the Word of God will not be of any effect in your life. The Bible will
be like any other book you read.

One of the signs of a baby is that the baby will cry for milk when he or she
is hungry. If the baby is not crying for milk either the baby is overfed or
something is wrong with the baby. When our oldest daughter was born,
for some reason she could not digest her mother's milk. She would just
cry and cry for hours and we did not know what the problem was until
we took her to the hospital. The milk she was drinking was not digesting
properly and she needed some additional help.

One of the signs of a true born-again experience is a hunger for the Word
of God. What is milk to a natural baby is the Word of God to a spiritual
baby. If a spiritual baby is not hungry for the Word of God, then their
born-again experience is questionable. You might have repeated a prayer
after someone, but if there was no true conviction of sin or revelation of
Jesus in your life, you need to hear the preaching of the gospel again.

The results of a recent survey done by Barna Research Group indicate
that many Christians are confused about their salvation. Christians don't
understand—or believe—their own theology about salvation. The Barna
Research Group asked 6,242 adults nationwide, "Can a good person earn
their way to heaven?" The percentages of those responding "yes" were as
follows:[1]

Assembly of God 22%

Baptist 38%

Presbyterian 52%

Lutheran 54%

Episcopalian 58%

Methodist 59%

[1] http://www.awmi.net/extra/article/new_you

Roman Catholic 82%

Another sign of a true born-again experience is the conviction of the Holy Spirit. When your spirit is born again it is very sensitive. When you do something wrong or disobey the Lord there will be a red light that goes on in your spirit. Actually, that is your spiritual conscience. Little things of the flesh, sin, or the world can bother you just like a baby is very sensitive to pain. A little harshness can make a baby cry.

Without parental support or support from an adult, a baby will never grow up healthy. A baby is not able to digest steak or apple pie. If you try to feed those to the baby, the baby will choke and die. Babyhood is when someone needs to do everything for you. In the spirit it is the same. Every spiritual child needs a spiritual parent. It does not matter at what age a person is saved. This is one of the greatest lacks in Christendom and, as a result, most Christians grow up defected or remain a spiritual baby for the rest of their lives.

We have untold numbers of babies being born into the Kingdom every day. The body of Christ is experiencing a tremendous shortage of spiritual parents who can take care of and disciple these new believers.

A baby who grows up without parents can develop lots of disorders and can become dangerous to society. Children who grow up in a single parent home may have difficulties coping with society during adolescence. A baby needs a father and a mother for its proper development. The nurturing, caring, and loving heart of a mother and the authoritative, forgiving, providing, protecting and leading nature of a father is a must for a baby's proper growth. In the church, God has appointed spiritual parents. He gave the five-fold ministers to equip or mature the saints for the work of the ministry.

> "And He Himself gave some to be apostles, some prophets,
> some evangelists, and some pastors and teachers."
> (Ephesians 4:11)

The above ministries are spiritual offices or departments. In the natural, each country is governed by a government, and the president or the prime minister appoints ministers to oversee different areas of the government.

He will appoint some to take care of transportation, energy, finances, international relations, welfare, etc. These ministers should be very reputable and will have certain authority that is not available to the common citizens. They are paid by the government.

The Kingdom of God is an invisible Kingdom. Jesus is the King of the Kingdom. The Church is the visible aspect of the invisible Kingdom and the five-fold ministry gifts are the governing body of the Kingdom. The Kingdom of God rules over the natural and earthly governments (Daniel 4:17,25,32). The spirit world is superior to the natural world: The natural world is governed by the spirit world.

A minister's job, contrary to what people often think, is not simply to go around and preach. They are directly appointed by Jesus to govern the Church. No person appoints or calls these people to ministry. That is why the Bible says specifically, "He Himself gave..." The next verse tells why He gave these ministry gifts to the Church.

> "*For the equipping of the saints* for the work of ministry, for the edifying of the body of Christ, till we all come to the unity of the faith and of the knowledge of the Son of God, to a perfect man, to the measure of the stature of the fullness of Christ; *that we should no longer be children...*" (Ephesians 4:12-14) (Italics added)

When you get born again you need people to pray for you, take care of you, and share the Word with you—explaining what the Bible is about, who God is, and how everything was created. You might hear people speaking in tongues and get confused or bewildered.

You will hear about giving tithes and offerings and you may not feel to give much because of selfishness. Know that children are naturally very selfish. Most spiritual things may not make any sense to you at this time. You will feel like you entered into a new world altogether because you have.

When you are a baby you do not change your diaper by yourself or take a bath by yourself. If you try to, though most babies think they can, you know what the result would be. That is the problem with the infancy stage. A baby does not have the maturity to know what he is and is not capable of doing.

A baby Christian might need the help of others to get clean. The right place to get help is a church that teaches the pure Word of God. Some new believers may need to go through some deliverance and emotional cleansing. Some of the most repeated words I hear from my three children are, "I can do it by myself," or, "I want to do it." As a parent you know they are not able to do certain things, but children somehow do not come with that kind of discernment. A baby Christian is not any different.

For some reason we think we can do it all by ourselves. So, we need to go through this process of messing up and cleaning up again and again. One incident usually will not teach us the lesson. The next time we are faced with an obstacle we will again be tempted to say, "I want to deal with it by myself."

A baby Christian might mess up many times and make the same mistakes again and again. It is natural for a baby to repeat the same mistake and get dirty. Even if a baby falls ten times a day trying to walk, we will not throw that baby outside. But, if after ten years the baby keeps falling every time he or she is trying to walk, then we need to seek some medical help. There is a problem if you are still making the same mistakes that you made when you first got saved. I would like to say to you, "It is time to grow up."

You do not like your children making the same mistake when they are ten that they used to make when they were three, do you? I want you to know that God is not upset when He sees baby Christians making a mistake because He knows they were just born and how much they are able to handle.

In childhood you gain skills and obtain knowledge. You discover that you still need adult supervision, help, or incentive to make you do things. Often, you need to be told to do something. You may look back and see what you did when you first got saved and may feel embarrassed or see how things needed to be changed in how you did them. I look back at what I preached 10 years ago and cannot believe that I preached that kind of stuff. Unfortunately, many stop in their spiritual childhood and never grow up to be a mature man in the spirit.

You read your Bible but may not have any clue how it is benefiting you. It is just like when I tell my five-year-old to brush his teeth twice a day or to eat his vegetables. He does not have any clue how it is helping him for the future. He would rather go without brushing his teeth and play some more. He just feels like that is a waste of time.

I must remind him, someday you will appreciate that Daddy compelled you to brush your teeth every day. It is the same with praying and reading the Bible. At this stage it may feel boring or a waste of time. But, if you keep up with it and develop those habits they will bring great returns later in life.

Adolescence in the spirit is where you try out different things, find out what your spiritual gifts are, and learn how to operate in them. You learn how to hear from God and develop your own style of prayer, fasting, etc. You will learn to share the gospel with others. In the natural our body goes through changes when we reach puberty. You know you possess reproductive ability, but you are not stable and do not have the maturity to handle such responsibility.

Most of the things you do will be based on emotions or feelings and as long as something excites you emotionally you will do it. That is the time the spiritual parents need to step in to encourage and motivate you to keep going. If this is happening to you now that means you lack maturity in spiritual things. Even mature Christians need encouragement at times.

Also, you will learn how to interpret the scriptures without getting too spooky. Now is when you have so much energy and want to help everybody in the world, but generally not for the right reasons or with the right heart. It is usually mostly for personal glory and fame. You want to be the greatest in the Kingdom and you believe you can do all things.

When we look at the lives of the disciples in the Gospels we can see these patterns. They went through this experience in three years with Jesus. They had to grow up fast in the spirit to continue the work of Jesus on this earth. One main difference between the natural and spiritual life is you can speed up the process in the spirit. It depends on how much time you invest. It can be a life-long process, and in a sense it is, but you can reach different heights in the spirit as you learn to cooperate with God.

Spiritual adolescence is the time that you learn quite a bit about everything and it is one of the most important seasons in your spiritual journey. Here you lay some key foundational stones in your life regarding your future walk with the Lord. This is the time you will begin to discover your purpose for your life. If you are not serious at this time and get side-tracked it will hinder your spiritual maturity, just like in adolescence many youth get side-tracked and it takes them a while to get back into their right mind.

Here you need strong but gentle spiritual mentors to guide you in the right direction and speak into your life about what you are going through. At this stage Christians make lots of mistakes in both personal life and public life and many backslide at this point because they either get disappointed in themselves, or are influenced by the world. I have found that there are more spiritual adolescents in the Church today than any other group.

Adulthood in the spirit is when you know how to recognize the voice of the Holy Spirit and you know how to interpret the scriptures and recognize the deception of the enemy. You do not need regular external influence or stimuli to get you to do anything spiritual. You have developed those spiritual habits and do them because you know you need them. The following two scriptures talk about spiritual adults:

1 John 2:13 says,

> "...I write to you, young men, because you have overcome the wicked one."

1 John 2:14 says,

> "...I have written to you, young men, because you are strong, and the Word of God abides in you, and you have overcome the wicked one."

In adulthood you can minister to others but may not be very effective because you lack experience, even though you may have the right information. In spiritual adulthood you put a lot of energy into what you are doing and you believe that if you do not prepare and give it your best shot, it is not a shot at all. It is all about what your strength and ability can produce.

These are the best volunteers because you can trust them with tasks and they will get them done. Also, they will be good team members and good soul-winners. One of the signs of maturity is the ability to reproduce. When you are mature in the spirit you need to win others to Christ. They are your spiritual children. Those who are spiritual adults are the pillars of a church and much of the ministry depends on their functioning. They can be good leaders in different committees and groups and governing bodies.

Marriage in the spirit is when you enter into a deeper level of relationship with the Holy Spirit and you walk in fellowship and communion with God all the time. Actually, it is a spiritual marriage and you cannot separate or go too long without having that sweet communion with God. It is a constant experience of walking with the Lord.

It is interesting here how different people develop relationships with different Persons of the Trinity. Some love the Holy Spirit and others love Jesus or the Father, and still others may have different dimensions of relationship with each in different seasons of their life. I believe it depends on their childhood experience as they were growing up.

Here you begin to minister to others on a deeper level. I would say, if you are called, you are ready to enter the ministry where you can teach, minister and serve for the edification of others. You develop a heart for other people and want to help them grow in the spirit and move them toward maturity in the Word. This is the best time for ministry and in your spiritual life because it is not you who does all these things, but God working *through* you to touch others.

After eighty years of life Moses entered this season at Mount Horeb. Until then he was being matured in different areas of his life and he was very faithful in what he was doing. At Mount Horeb he had a revelation of God, which he had never before experienced. Let me tell you, the revelation you have of God determines your victory over the enemy. Each new season brings a new revelation of God that you did not have before. Each assignment from God comes with a new revelation of God. Your prosperity depends on your personal revelation of God.

Moses entered into a deeper level of intimacy with God that he never had before. God began to speak to him regularly, face-to-face, and fellowship with him. He received a new assignment for his life, to go to Egypt, but the task was so big that his natural strength was not enough to deliver the people from slavery. God was doing the work for him and Moses was just a representative of God.

This is what I call the real ministry. Moses spoke only what God wanted him to speak and did only what God wanted him to do. Jesus said the same thing about His life, that He does only what He sees His Father doing and speaks only what He hears from the Father.

> "...Most assuredly I say to you, the Son can do nothing of Himself, but what He sees the Father do; for whatever He does, the Son also does in like manner." (John 5:19)

> "...and the word which you hear is not Mine but the Father's who sent Me." (John 14:24)

This takes the pressure off and you enter into a rest that is promised by God for all believers. Ministry is not doing your work or having a great program, but doing the work of the One who called you and saying what He wants you to say. God wants each of His children to enter into this realm and take His glory wherever they go.

Spiritual mid-life is the point in your life where you decide if you want to go further with God or get settled. It is a time of crisis just like the mid-life crisis in the natural. There is no limit with God but your health and body have limits. If you are not careful you can make big mistakes in this season. You are successful now and you have other people serving you and helping you.

David made a big mistake in his life during this time. He became a great king and was very successful and had everything he needed. He used to go to war and fight, but for some reason he got complacent and stayed back at the palace where he was tempted, and committed adultery. This season can be a great blessing and it does not have to be a crisis at all if you continue to do that which helped you to get to this point. You can continue to grow in God and enjoy more depth of His love and fellowship.

Spiritual old age is when you become more of a spiritual mentor and have a wealth of experience to share and teach others. It is very rare to find such people. What makes a person your Father or Mother in the spirit? First, they might have begotten you in the spirit or imparted some spiritual truth into your life. Also, they will have a lot of wisdom and insight into spiritual things. A person does not need to be old in the natural to be a spiritual father or a mentor. They will know God's ways and understand how He operates.

1 John 2:13 says,

> "I write to you, fathers, because you have known Him who is from the beginning."

> "Those who are planted in the house of the LORD shall flourish in the courts of our God. They shall still bear fruit in old age; they shall be fresh and flourishing." (Psalm 92:13-14)

Spiritual fathers may have many spiritual children and grandchildren. They will become a spiritual consultant where those who are young in the spirit can come and receive counsel and correction.

You can discern and know what stage you are at in your Christian life. Ask God to help you mature and become a spiritual parent. Cry out and ask God to help you win souls into the Kingdom. The body of Christ needs your help. There are people waiting to be discipled by you. Jesus said to go and make disciples of all nations. Recognize which season you are at in your life and seek the right help to reach the next stage.

In the natural, one season gives birth to another season. In India where I grew up, we have four seasons, but it feels like we have only two seasons; summer and monsoon, because of the humidity and heat. When I came to the US, one thing I enjoyed very much was the change of seasons and I learned how the four seasons work with distinctive characteristics and weather patterns.

If you look at the Jewish calendar it is somewhat run according to the four seasons. The springtime is the New Year on the Jewish calendar. Before the spring comes, the winter kind of causes everything to appear dead though great life is hidden in trees and plants.

Before a new beginning, something must die in our life. One season gives birth to the next season in the natural. And, one season must come to an end before the beginning of a new one. It is the same in the spirit. One season must end before a new season begins. Very often seasons may end with great pain. Entering into a new season is like having a baby. When a baby is being birthed there is great pain involved. You cannot have a new baby without going through the pain of birth.

The transition from one season to another is a slow process. When it reaches fall, it is kind of sad to watch all the leaves falling from the trees. Those leaves will never get a chance to live again. They are dead and separated from the trees forever. We should be willing to let go of the past season in order to enter into a new season in the spirit. Whatever is dead needs to be separated and buried forever.

God wants you to know about His timing and how to discern your season. Time and season in the spirit realm are more real than the natural realm's time and season. Whether you are running a business, leading a church, or the head of an organization or family, your success depends upon your ability to discern the time and new seasons in the spirit and how to take initiative in bringing about necessary change. Your success depends on your ability to know when God is taking you, your business, church, organization, or family into a new season.

Our enemy is also aware of God's timing and seasons. He will try his best to push you ahead of God's timing or slow you down so you miss God's timing. Many people fail because they step ahead of God or they wait around too long and do not take action when the time comes. We succeed only when we move in step with Him discerning His time and seasons.

In the next few chapters we are going to study the signs God uses to communicate His timing to us. Many of us have to go through some struggles before we learn to recognize His timing. We do not easily understand His ways and His timing. We need to mature in hearing His voice daily in our lives. It does not happen that easy and on the way we unfortunately make some mistakes. Welcome to the club!

Chapter 3

WAYS GOD COMMUNICATES HIS TIMING

"God does speak — sometimes one way and sometimes another — even though people may not understand it." Job 33:14 (NCV)

GOD HAS SPECIFIC SEASONS FOR YOUR LIFE. Each of those seasons begins with signs and characteristics that are unique. He reveals His purpose concerning your life in progressive stages.

Nature has four seasons; spring, summer, fall and winter. Each of these seasons has specific signs and expressions. Each season is different from the others. Nature goes through a series of changes at the end and beginning of each season. By looking at the signs and changes that are occurring, you can recognize which season is ending and which is beginning.

The changing of a season does not occur at one particular point in time. This occurs over a period of time in which one season comes to an end and another one emerges. Seasonal change can be focused around a particular event or a moment, but it will always take a period of time to end one season and begin another.

For example, in the natural when we go from one season to another it is always a slow change and it may take days or weeks to noticeably begin a new season. But, our calendars note a particular date and time as the beginning of a new season. Similarly, in the spirit when we go from one season to another it is a process rather than a particular event, though it might be marked by a particular event.

When you and I end a season in our lives and enter a new season, there are signs and changes that take place in our lives. Each new season in life starts with its own specific signs. All seasons do not start the same way. God uses different ways to usher in a new season. If we learn to recognize those changes and signs, we can know the times and seasons of our lives.

Jesus said in Matthew 16:2-3,

> "At sunset you say we will have good weather, because the sky is red. And in the morning you say that it will be a rainy day, because the sky is dark and red. You see these signs in the sky and know what they mean. In the same way, you see the things that I am doing now, but you don't know their meaning." (NCV)

In the above scripture Jesus was revealing a secret to knowing times and seasons. He was saying that if we notice the change that is taking place in the atmosphere, then we can predict the weather in the natural. Similarly, if we notice the things God is doing in our lives, there are signs that tell us the seasons in the spirit. These signs will help us recognize the time of a new season in the spirit.

Jesus was comparing natural timing with spiritual timing. The people knew how to notice the elements of the sky and earth and tell the time in the natural, but they had no clue how to discern the spiritual time they were in. The same can happen to us if we do not know how to discern God's timing based on what we are going through in our natural circumstances.

Many in the body of Christ do not fulfill their purpose because they do not know how to recognize God's timing and move accordingly. Either they step ahead of God's timing, or they lag behind. The reason many are not in the season God wants them to be in is because they do not know how to interpret the signs of the spiritual seasons based on their natural circumstances. We need to learn how to be in step with God for each area of life.

One of the reasons you may not be happy is because you are not in the season God wants you to be in. For every purposeful event in life, there is a specific timing. Many marry the right person at the wrong time and face a lot of challenges. Then, they think they married the wrong person. No, you have not married the wrong person, but you may have married in the wrong season of your life.

It may seem like you are going through two seasons of your life at the same time. This is often the reason that you are faced with challenges. You were not created to go through two seasons at the same time. Imagine nature going through summer and winter at the same time. It would be chaotic. But, if you humble yourself and seek God, He will give you the grace and help you need.

When God is getting ready to unfold His next season in our lives, He will send one of the seven signs to our lives. If we are to keep moving in the seasons of God for our lives, then we need to learn how to hear His voice. There are different ways God speaks to us and we should not limit Him to one particular way. While there are seven signs of a new season, there are eight ways God uses to communicate His timing. There are more ways God uses to speak to us generally, but I have limited it to eight regarding this particular subject. **Collectively, I am calling them the first sign God uses to communicate His timing to us.**

1) HIS WORD

There are at least 525 instances in the Bible where God directly spoke to people. This is without counting Him speaking through dreams, visions, angels or prophets. The Word of God is the foundation of Christian life. God communicates His universal will through His Word. He can also communicate His specific will and timing through His Word. He can inspire the written Word through His Holy Spirit and it can be an answer or guide to our next season in life.

One of the primary ways God communicates His timing to a believer is through His Word. We need to develop a daily habit of spending time reading and meditating on His Word. Most of the time, the Holy Spirit brings to our remembrance the Word that is already planted in our heart. If our heart is empty of His Word, then He cannot lead us by His Word.

When you are not sure of the source of the voice you hear in your heart, the best thing to do is to wait upon God. This may raise the question of how to wait upon Him. And, what do you do when you wait upon Him? There are three major words used in the Hebrew language that teach us about waiting on God. Waiting on God can mean different things in different situations.

The first word used is 'qavah' (Strong's H6960) which means to wait, to look for, hope, or expect. (Psalm 25:21, 27:14)

The second word is 'damam' (Strong's H1826) which means to be silent, be still, be dumb. This also means to rest. (Psalm 37:7a)

The third word used in Hebrew is 'shamar' (Strong's H8104) which means to keep, guard, observe, protect, preserve.

There are times when waiting on God is all you feel led to do. You wait in His presence until you receive an answer from Him. You will worship and praise Him and meditate on His Word. At other times you wait on Him in complete silence. He may want you to rest in His presence to calm your flesh and mind in order to hear from Him. You will not say anything or read anything, just wait on Him. In the third type of waiting, you continue with your daily routine and your spirit is waiting on Him. You will do all of the above and still continue with your normal life. Whichever way suits you the best will be based on the intensity of the situation you are facing at the time.

God's Word contains the solutions to every problem we will ever face. The

Bible says His Word is a lamp unto our feet and a light unto our path (Psalm 119:105). In Jeremiah's life, new seasons started when the Word of the LORD came to him. Jeremiah 1:4-5 says,

> "Then the word of the Lord came to me, saying: "Before I formed you in the womb I knew you; before you were born I sanctified you; I ordained you a prophet to the nations."

The Word of the Lord will come to you unexpectedly and you need to be open to receive it and run with it. It may not make sense in the natural, but know that all things are possible with the Lord. You may hear from the Lord either when reading His Word, through His Holy Spirit, through a preacher or friend, or even, though rarely, through an angel.

When you receive a word from the Lord it is like a woman who is pregnant with a baby. You feel a stirring in your spirit. There is an expectancy in your spirit as if God is about to do something on your behalf. Before God does something in our lives, He will cause a stirring that will make us really uncomfortable in many ways. We may feel nothing good is happening outwardly but God may be doing something powerful for us in the spirit in the midst of that stirring.

Many times, we miss God's season in our lives because when God speaks to us we do not believe it. It may seem impossible in the natural and beyond your abilities. So, He will introduce some circumstances to bring us to the place where we will believe that word beyond a shadow of a doubt. When we receive the word our response should be as that of Mary who said, "Behold the maidservant of the Lord! Let it be to me according to your word." (Luke 1:38)

Another problem with many is not that they do not believe what God says but they do not know what to do after they receive a word from God. There is a specific time for each of God's promises to be fulfilled in your life. I explain in detail about what to do after you receive a word from the Lord in the *Faith and God's Timing* chapter.

A new season started in Abraham's life in the Old Testament when he heard a word from the Lord. The Lord told him to get out of his country and away from his father's house to a land that He would show him. Abraham started his journey without knowing where he was going. The Bible says in Hebrews 11:8,

> "By faith Abraham obeyed when he was called to go out to the place which he would receive as an inheritance. And he went out, not knowing where he was going."

2) THE HOLY SPIRIT

This is one of the main ways God communicates with His children, but it takes training and experience to recognize the voice of the Holy Spirit in your spirit. Every single believer hears the voice of God in their spirit. The goal is for each believer to hear the voice of God, but it takes time to develop and discern God's voice. It is not because God is not speaking that we do not hear. Recognizing His voice is the real test. We will make mistakes more than once but we will grow from glory to glory.

We need to learn how to differentiate between strong feelings and the voice of the Spirit. The voice of the Spirit is a gentle and still voice but it will be steady in our heart. Usually, it does not increase or decrease in volume. The feelings and the voices of the flesh fluctuate in volume and excitement as time goes by. Sometimes it is an impression, a picture in our heart, an inspiration, or we feel a small push in our spirit.

There are three voices we hear in our hearts. One is the voice of the flesh. The second one is the voice of the devil. And, the third is the voice of the Spirit in our spirit. One of the ways to detect the voices is to wait on God's presence. The voices of the flesh and the devil will diminish in time as you seek God. The voice of the Spirit will remain the same even if days go by. I have learned from experience that there is no decision in your life where God does not have the time to speak to you. Sometimes what we think is an emergency is not an emergency at all, but merely the build-up of our fleshly feelings. Others may pressure you to make a decision but you need to take time to hear from God for yourself.

One of the main responsibilities of the Holy Spirit is to guide us in truth. He is the Spirit of Truth and He is here to teach and lead us. Every spirit-filled Christian can hear from God. That is why the Bible says, "Those who are led by the Spirit are the children of God" (Romans 8:14). We are not supposed to be led only by other means, like preachers or prophets. It is dangerous for a spirit-filled Christian to persistently be led only by prophets or other people. Jesus said His sheep hear His voice and follow Him (John 10:27).

In order to be led by His Spirit we need to be walking in obedience to His Word. I believe if we are to be led by His Spirit we need to fill our heart with His Word. The Holy Spirit always works in obedience to the Word of God. Where there is no Word, there is no Spirit. The Holy Spirit comes to fulfill the Word of God (Luke 1:35). The Holy Spirit comes to confirm the Word of God which is spoken (Mark 16:20). The Holy Spirit and the Word of God always work in agreement. The Holy Spirit will never contradict the written Word.

One of the reasons God sent the Holy Spirit is to show us the will of God. In truth, the Holy Spirit is the only One who always knows God's will and timing concerning our lives. The Bible says that no one knows what is in our heart except our spirit. In the same way, no one knows what is in God's heart except the Spirit of God.

> "For what man knows the things of a man except the spirit of the man which is in him? Even so no one knows the things of God except the Spirit of God." (1 Corinthians 2:11)

The Holy Spirit was present when God designed and planned each of our lives in eternity. Jesus said when the Spirit of Truth comes He will lead us into all truth (John 16:13). The Bible says no eye has seen nor ear heard what God has prepared for those who love Him, but His Holy Spirit has revealed that to us.

> "But as it is written: "Eye has not seen, nor ear heard, nor have entered into the heart of man the things which God has prepared for those who love Him. But God has revealed them to us through His Spirit..." (1 Corinthians 2:9 & 10)

In the Gospel of Luke we read of Simeon, who was led by the Holy Spirit concerning God's timing for his life. He was told that he would not die until he saw the Christ.

Luke 2:25-27 says,

> "And behold, there was a man in Jerusalem whose name was Simeon, and this man was just and devout, waiting for the Consolation of Israel, and the Holy Spirit was upon him. And it had been revealed to him by the Holy Spirit that he would not see death before he had seen the Lord's Christ. So he came by the Spirit into the temple."

3) DREAMS

We see in the Bible that God used dreams to communicate His timing to people. He used dreams both in the Old and New Testaments (Genesis 41; Matthew 2:13). In Job we read that He uses dreams to communicate to us.

Job 33:14-16 says,

> "For God may speak in one way, or in another, yet man does not perceive it. In a dream, in a vision of the night, when deep sleep falls upon men, while slumbering on their beds, then He opens the ears of men, and seals their instruction."

This is not a book about dreams but I want to give you some basic understanding about them and how they play a role in Christian's lives. There are two major kinds of dreams we have while we sleep. One is a *hearing* dream and the second is a *seeing* dream. The first type is when God or someone else communicates a message and you hear it in your dream. When you have a hearing dream you need to pay close attention to what you hear because what you hear is the actual message being communicated to you.

In Matthew's Gospel, God spoke to Joseph three times concerning His timing and new season using this particular type of dream.

Matthew 1:20-24 says,

> "But while he thought about these things, behold, an angel of the Lord appeared to him in a dream, saying, "Joseph, son of David, do not be afraid to take to you Mary your wife, for that which is conceived in her is of the Holy Spirit. And she will bring forth a Son, and you shall call His name Jesus, for He

will save His people from their sins." So all this was done that it might be fulfilled which was spoken by the Lord through the prophet, saying: "Behold, the virgin shall be with child, and bear a Son, and they shall call His name Immanuel," which is translated, "God with us." Then Joseph, being aroused from sleep, did as the angel of the Lord commanded him and took to him his wife."

You can find other examples in Matthew 2:13-14 & 19:2.

The second kind of dream is when you see the message in pictures; impressions, things, people, places and incidents, and you may or may not hear any sound or voice. This type of dream is divided into three groups; dreams of the mind, dreams of the flesh and dreams of the spirit. All dreams we see are not from God or the enemy. Dreams of the mind are dreams you see based on what you were going through emotionally at a particular time and may not mean anything (Ecclesiastes 5:3).

Dreams of the flesh are those you see about the nature of your flesh and sometimes can also be influenced by the enemy. Dreams of the spirit are those from God or the enemy that communicate with our spirit either about His plans, or to reveal the plans of the enemy. The dreams that come to you from God will be in color and the dreams about the enemy you will see in black and white or in gray.

Usually, the people, places, incidents, objects, or anything you see in dreams, visions and trances have metaphoric meaning. What is a metaphor? A metaphor is a figure of speech in which a word or phrase literally denoting one kind of object or idea is used in place of another to suggest a likeness or analogy between them (Merriam Webster). The actual meaning or message of the dream may have nothing to do with what you see in the dream.

For example, if you see a snake in your dream, that may have nothing to do with an actual snake. A snake usually represents the devil, deception, a lie or an attack of the enemy. You can know these by what the snake was doing in the dream. Do not take literally what you see in your dream. You need to interpret it with the help of the Holy Spirit and with the wisdom of God. What you see in dreams are not actual pictures of what is going to happen. I have seen people who took their dream literally and ended up in trouble.

That means what you see in your dream will have nothing to do with the actual objects you see. That may sound confusing. The best way to know this is to study the dreams in the Bible. Let me explain it a little bit here. You remember Joseph's dream. First, he saw the sheaves. The sheaves represented him and his brothers (Genesis 37:7). Seeing a dog in your dream does not mean the next day you need to go out and get a puppy. It might be showing you to watch out for people who have the nature of a dog or a warning to correct some flaws in your own life (Philippians 3:2).

Pharaoh dreamed about seven lean cows and seven fat cows. They actually symbolized the seven years of plenty and seven years of famine that were to come. Dreams come most often in symbols or in pictures and you need to know how to interpret them. Seldom will a dream actually mean exactly what you see. Spiritual dreams contain a hidden meaning and typology. This is similar to the parables Jesus shared in the Gospels.

When God wanted Peter to go and minister to Gentiles He showed him a picture of a sheet coming down from heaven with all kinds of unclean animals and creatures. He told Peter to take them and eat. If you interpret that naturally, you need to go out and find some unclean animals and eat them raw. That would be foolish. That vision had a spiritual meaning behind it. God will always show you something you can relate to or things or places with which you are familiar. Daniel saw goats and leopards coming out of the water. They were symbols of world leaders and heads of nations, not actual animals in the forest. The best way to interpret a dream is to ask the Holy Spirit to give you wisdom to understand and gradually He will unfold the meaning.

I had an interesting dream as we were packing and getting ready to move from Denver, Colorado. We had a car that did not have any dents or scratches though we used it for two years. One night I had a dream that a bull came and hit the back panel of my car on the right side. That was a *seeing* dream. When I woke up, that dream stayed with me and I wondered how a bull could ever come and hit the back of my car. There was no chance in the natural for that to happen.

Two days later, as I was backing out of the garage to go somewhere, I hit another car that was parked outside the garage. Usually, there is no one parked outside our garage. This was someone who came to visit us that morning. The exact spot that I saw in my dream was damaged and it was the worst damage we ever had to our car. If only I had prayed for the interpretation of that dream—the enemy's plan would have been destroyed and my car would have been dent free!

Find the references about dreams and visions in the Bible. Learn what people actually saw and what the dreams meant, and you will have a basic foundation about how dreams work and how to interpret them. My purpose here is not to teach you how to interpret dreams. There are books and resources available that you can read to learn more about that subject.

We see in the Bible that God communicates through dreams both to His people and to heathens about His timing. In Genesis we read of Pharaoh's dream concerning the plentiful years followed by the drought (Genesis 41:1-8). But, it takes a child of God to interpret Heaven-sent dreams. God used Joseph in Egypt to interpret the dream and as a result he was used as an instrument to bring that dream into fulfillment. In the book of Daniel we read about another heathen king who had a dream from God (Daniel 2:1). God used Daniel to interpret the dream and as a result he was promoted in the kingdom.

4) VISIONS

Dreaming is something which happens while we sleep, but visions can happen while we are asleep or awake. Sometimes while in prayer or in the presence of God in worship, God will open up the spirit world and show us what is happening or going to happen. God uses dreams to communicate truths or events personally related to us regarding His timing. He uses visions more frequently to reveal His timing regarding ministry or world events or changes. God used visions in the Bible to communicate future events of earth and end time events. Below are two examples of how God communicated His timing through visions.

Acts 11:5-9 says,

> "I was in the city of Joppa praying; and in a trance I saw a vi-

sion, an object descending like a great sheet, let down from heaven by four corners; and it came to me. When I observed it intently and considered, I saw four-footed animals of the earth, wild beasts, creeping things, and birds of the air. And I heard a voice saying to me, 'Rise, Peter; kill and eat.' But I said, 'Not so, Lord! For nothing common or unclean has at any time entered my mouth.' But the voice answered me again from heaven, 'What God has cleansed you must not call common.'"

Acts 16:9 says,

"And a vision appeared to Paul in the night. A man of Macedonia stood and pleaded with him, saying, "Come over to Macedonia and help us.""

5) ANGELS

Angels are God's messengers. We see in the Bible that oftentimes angels came and communicated God's will and timing to people. An angel appeared to Gideon in the book of Judges and told him what he was supposed to do (Judges 6:11-23). When the fullness of time came for the Son of God to be born on this earth, God sent an angel to a woman called Mary in Nazareth and spoke to her about the plan God had for her life (Luke 1:26-38). I do not see in the Bible that she was expecting an angel or a word from the Lord. She entered a new season in her life because of the word she received from God.

6) SIGNS, WONDERS AND MIRACLES

This is another means God uses to show His plan and purpose to people. Whenever a sign, wonder or miracle occurred it was God revealing His will and timing concerning a situation to the people witnessing the event. When Jesus turned the water into wine at the wedding of Cana, the Bible says He manifested His glory and His disciples believed in Him (John 2:11).

Acts 2:18-21 says,

"And on My menservants and on My maidservants I will pour out My Spirit in those days; and they shall prophesy. I will show *wonders* in heaven above and *signs* in the earth beneath: Blood and fire and vapor of smoke. The sun shall be turned into darkness, and the moon into blood, *before the coming of the great and awesome day of the Lord.* And it shall come to pass that whoever calls on the name of the Lord shall be saved." (Italics added)

7) PROPHECY/PROPHETIC PREACHING

This is another way God reveals His timing. When the Word of God comes alive through anointed preaching, God's will or timing for your life is communicated to you. Many times there is confirmation as to why you are going through what you are going through. God can send a man or woman to tell you specifically what you should do or not do in a particular situation.

The ministry of John the Baptist is an example of how God communicates His timing through prophetic preaching. He was a prophet and came preaching the baptism of repentance as a forerunner to Jesus. He was preparing people for the new spiritual season they would enter with the coming of Jesus.

8) PRAYER

Prayer is communication with God. Communion comes as a result of communication. Jesus spent many nights with the Father alone in prayer while He was doing His earthly ministry. His relationship with His Father through prayer helped Him to know the timing for His ministry. If the Son of God had to do that to fulfill His purpose, how much more do we have to do it in our lives? As I mentioned above, Peter, receiving the vision while he was praying about the ministry to the Gentiles, is a clear example of knowing God's timing through prayer.

Most people use prayer only to tell God their needs. That is not the whole purpose of prayer. God communicates with us through prayer. He shows us His plans and tells us what to do, what not to do and when to do it.

There are different kinds of prayers in the Bible. In chapter five of Ephesians, we read about praying with all prayers. The most effective form of prayer is when God talks to you more than you talk to Him. God loves to talk to us and He is always willing to talk to us. Prayer combined with fasting is another effective way, but always obey the leading of the Holy Spirit in fasting. Unless He tells you, do not start a lengthy fast.

Chapter 4

ADVERSITY AND GOD'S TIMING

"...Those who are wise will find a time and a way to do what is right,

for there is a time and a way for everything, even when a person is in trouble."
Ecclesiastes 8:5-6 (NLT)

THE SECOND SIGN BY WHICH WE KNOW WE ARE ENTERING A NEW SEASON IN OUR LIVES IS GOD ALLOWING US TO GO THROUGH SOME TRIALS AND ADVERSITIES. This is a painful way of knowing God's timing and we all go through it at times. In the Gospel of John we read about the pool of Bethesda. There was something miraculous about this pool. It was a pool of healing. I believe that this story speaks more clearly about God's timing than any other. There was a great multitude of sick people around this pool waiting for the moving of the water (John 5:2-4).

An angel came and stirred up the water in a certain time and the first person who stepped into the pool got healed of any disease or sickness.

> "For an angel went down at a certain time into the pool, and stirred up the water; then whoever stepped in first, after the stirring of the water, was made well of whatever disease he had." (John 5:4)

That means your healing depended on your ability to know when the angel was coming to stir the water next. Everyone's healing depended on the timing. God was not being partial. He gave everyone an equal opportunity to get healed. Timing was everything for their healing.

Imagine that you were at that pool waiting for your healing. You knew you could get healed but you did not know when the angel would come. It could be at midnight or early morning or lunchtime.

One thing to learn from this story is that God does not operate according to our need or when we want Him to, but according to His timing. Our breakthroughs depend on our ability to recognize His timing. We need to notice in the above scripture that it was an angel of God who came and troubled the water. It was supernatural and man was not in control of it. We are not in control of everything that happens in our lives.

Sometimes God moves at times when we least expect Him to or in ways we are not familiar with. When you know how to recognize your season in the spirit, your life will never be the same again. I want to teach this principle from the Word of God so you will be prepared and ready when the next season in your life arrives.

It is interesting to notice that the people needed to wait for the stirring of the water. In the King James Version the word used is "troubled," instead of stirring.

> "For an angel went down at a certain season into the pool, and troubled the water, whosoever the first after the troubling of the water stepped in was made whole of whatsoever disease he had." (John 5:4)

If there was no troubling; there was no healing. If anyone stepped into the water before the water was troubled; there was no healing. The word used for troubled in the Greek is *'tarasso'* (Strong's G5015), which means: to agitate; to cause one inward commotion; take away his calmness of mind; to disquiet; make restless; to trouble; to strike one's spirit with fear and dread; to render anxious or distressed.

The enemy can sense God's timing and he will try to distract us by various means, some I mention below, so we will miss our new season. He wants us to react and respond to these circumstances in the flesh. As long as we do that we will remain ineffective for God on this earth. The enemy will cause a trial, crisis, strained relationships, restlessness, loss of work, failure, stress, unexpected setbacks, financial crisis, betrayal, challenging circumstances, unplanned delays, or *anything that makes you feel that your present life has come to an end.* Any of these can be a sign that you are about to enter into a new season in your life.

When you face any of the above in your life beware, the enemy is trying to side-track you from God's purpose and timing and you need to be vigilant. I have seen this work over and over again in the Bible and in my life. When the enemy comes we need to be patient and hold on to what God said. He will avenge us and the very thing the enemy meant for evil and our destruction He will turn around and make work for our good. When God avenges us over our enemy we will walk away with our plunder or blessings.

Each aspect of our lives has different seasons. Our financial life has different seasons. Marriage has different seasons and stages. Professional life has different seasons and stages. If you are in ministry or business, you will go through different stages of growth and changes.

If your financial life has come to a crossroad and you are at the brink of bankruptcy or financial breakthrough, you may have arrived at the threshold of the next season in your financial life. The Holy Spirit may speak to your heart to do something radical in the area of giving and your obedience to that leading determines your next financial season. I share more about this in the *Sowing and God's Timing* chapter.

If your marriage has reached a tough spot and you feel there is no more excitement or hope, it is a sign that God wants to take the relationship in your marriage to a new level. You may have to humble yourself and seek some wise counsel in order to receive some new knowledge and skills to develop a better relationship. Many quit as soon as they face a critical stage in their marriage and never enter into their new season.

If professional life, ministry, church, or business has reached a place where you feel like everything has come to a plateau or end, and it seems like there is no future, that may be a stirring from the Lord to start something new in your life. You may need to do some redefining and restructuring to get where you need to be.

Watch for this and you will notice when God is getting ready to take you into a new season in your life. Be careful because this is also the time when many believers make mistakes. When they go through a trial in their lives they will go to fight with people thinking they are the ones who are causing it. They totally miss it, and the enemy is happy each time this happens because we are distracted and our energy is spent fighting battles with those from whom they did not originate with weapons that are not designed by God, instead of seeking the seasons of God.

It is just like the mother eagle who stirs up its nest to make the eaglets fly. As long as the nest is peaceful the eaglets will never take the risk to fly. It is no different with us. When God gets ready to do something new in our lives, there will be a stirring that will disturb our normal lives in many ways.

We need to discern at this moment whether what we are going through is caused by the enemy or is part of the maturing process of Christian life; or perhaps because of disobedience, pride, ignorance or sin in our lives. If God is allowing something to happen it is a waste of time to fight the enemy. Some do not believe that Christians will go through any negative circumstances unless they disobey God or the devil attacks them. That is not true. To the contrary, anyone who does the will of God will go through fiery trials in their lives.

The New Testament teaches that there are nine kinds of troubles and challenges a believer in Christ may go through. We will not all go through all of them. These are: **1)** persecution, Matthew 5:10; **2)** tribulation, John 16:33; Acts 14:22; **3)** the chastening of the Lord, Hebrews 12:5-6; **4)** various trials, James 1:2; **5**) temptations, James 1:12; **6**) reveling/reproaches, Matthew 5:11; **7**) suffering, Philippians 1:29; **8**) afflictions, 2 Corinthians 4:17; and **9**) martyrdom, Matthew 10:21; Luke 21:16.

We will face these things not when we have sinned or disobey God, but in our everyday Christian life. We may face any one of these prior to entering a new season in our lives. These are things God allows a believer to go through in this life. One of the reasons He allows us to go through these is to teach us how to recognize His timing. There are other reasons He allows us to go through these and I extensively explain them in my soon to be published book, "*Spiritual Tests*."

The Bible says these trials will come from five different sources. They are; the world system (John 16:33; Romans 5:3-4), the enemy (1 Peter 5:8), people (Matthew 5:11-12; 2 Corinthians 11:26), God (Hebrews 12:5-11), and our sinful nature (Galatians 5:17). Discernment is required to know the origin of each problem we are facing in our lives. Many times we get defeated and do not make progress in our life because we are misguided by the enemy about the real source of the problem or the battle.

As author Warren Wiersbe said, "You cannot control the origin of your suffering, but you can control the outcome" (from Strategy of Satan by Warren W. Wiersbe).When God is the source of our trial the best thing to do is to ask Him for its purpose and yield to it. Do not fight back. He will turn each adversity into an advantage for us. We see that in Saul's life before he became Paul, on his way to Damascus (Acts 9:1-6). When people are the source of your trial do not fight back either, but bless them (Romans 12:14). If you discern the enemy is using them, fight the real source. If the world and its systems fight against you the only thing that will overcome this world is your faith (1 John 5:4).

Sometimes God allows the enemy to bring trials to our lives, or to tempt us as He did in the cases of Job (Job 1:12), Jesus (Matthew 4:1), Peter (Luke 22:31-32), and Paul (2 Corinthians 12:7). With each trial He will provide the grace to go through or endure it. If the enemy is behind the trial you are facing, withstand and fight the battle. He may use people and worldly systems to fight against us but they are his tools and not the source. We must fight the source to win the battle.

To understand the purpose of the problem we face we need the wisdom of God. What brought the people mentioned in the Bible through their problem was the wisdom of God. The wisdom of God is the most powerful weapon against the enemy. We often look for the miracle or the breakthrough to come out of the trial. Before God did any miracle in the Bible He always manifested His wisdom.

That is why the Bible says to rejoice when you face challenges and hardships, because they are producing some good fruit in your life that otherwise would not be produced. James 1:2-4 says,

> "My brethren, count it all joy when you fall into various trials, knowing that the testing of your faith produces patience. But let patience have its perfect work, that you may be perfect and complete, lacking nothing."

The Bible does not say we need to whine and complain when we go through various trials. Unless we go through them we will not grow in our faith and patience. When we have patience we will be perfect, complete and lack nothing.

The next verse says, "If any of you lacks wisdom, let him ask of God, who gives to all liberally and without reproach, and it will be given to him" (James 1:5). That means when you are going through trials and testing and do not understand the purpose of it, ask God for wisdom and He will show you the reason. Most of us do not rejoice when we go through trials because we do not understand their reason, their purpose and the benefits they bring to us.

In the next chapter, Individuals and *God's Timing*, we will study in detail how great men of faith in the Bible went through trials and crises as they fulfilled the purpose of God for their lives. Crisis in our lives is not the absence of God but often a divinely orchestrated opportunity to manifest His glory. I have heard that in some languages in the world, the word *crisis* actually means *opportunity*.

The first miracle Jesus ever did was at a wedding in Cana. The family who was hosting the party ran out of wine. Anyone could imagine the emotional state of the family and the guests. Jesus was right there in person and that did not stop the family from going through that crisis.

The Bible says Jesus manifested His glory for the first time to His disciples by converting the water into wine and blessing that family (John 2:11). We see another incident when Jesus and His disciples were traveling in a boat. A great storm came and their lives were in danger. Jesus was sleeping in the boat right in their midst. They woke Jesus up and He rebuked the storm (Mark 4:35-41).

When the Israelites came out of Egypt they followed the leading of the presence of God through the cloud by day and the fire by night. On the third day they encountered a crisis in their midst. They ran out of water and food. Did God know that was going to happen? Of course He did. He wanted them to know that man shall not live by bread alone but by every word that proceeds from the mouth of God (Deuteronomy 8:2).

God manifested His glory in the wilderness by giving them water (Exodus 15:22-25). I could go on mentioning examples from the Bible of how people faced challenges and crises as they walked out the plan of God for their lives. It was not because they did not have enough faith but because this was part of the plan. Joseph, Moses, David, Esther, Ruth, and Daniel are just a few examples of people who faced challenging circumstances before they entered into a new season.

Some challenges are sent by God. When God is stirring the waters in your life, it is useless to fight the devil. Each time we enter into a new season we will be tested and troubled in different areas of life. God wants us to go to the next level in our walk with Him where we know Him more intimately than ever before.

We like the stories of Daniel, Shadrach, Meshach, and Abed-Nego in the book of Daniel. We are fascinated by the influential lives they lived and the impact they made in the kingdoms where they were living. Sometimes we forget the lion's den, the test, and the fire they went through just before they were promoted to higher positions.

Once you are faced with such challenges the question is, what will you do next? You need to set aside some time to seek the Lord concerning that matter, to know the source of the challenge and why it is happening.

Know this for sure, nothing happens in our lives without a reason and a specific purpose. Listen to Him carefully and do what He says. The Bible says, "Are any of you suffering hardships? You should pray." (James 5:13)

Seek counsel from people who are mature in the things of the spirit. When Nehemiah heard the news about Jerusalem's broken and destroyed wall, he did not abruptly resign from his job and run to Jerusalem.

The first thing he did was set aside a few days to fast and pray (Nehemiah 1:4-11). God gave him favor with the king. When you go through the challenge, you need to recognize with whom God gives you favor. God takes us to the next season in our lives by giving us favor with people of influence.

When Daniel's comrades plotted against him and influenced the king to write a decree saying anyone who prayed to any God other than the king for thirty days would be cast into a lion's den, the first thing he did was to pray. Daniel 6:10 says,

"Now when Daniel knew that the writing was signed, he went home. And in his upper room, with his windows open toward Jerusalem, he knelt down on his knees three times that day, and prayed and gave thanks before his God, as was his custom since early days."

When Paul and Silas were cast into the prison for preaching the gospel, the Bible says at midnight they began to *pray* and sing praises to God. Again, the first thing they did was pray.

"But at midnight Paul and Silas were praying and singing hymns to God, and the prisoners were listening to them." (Acts 16:25)

Nothing will work without prayer, and when nothing else is working, prayer will work.

From the incidents and people mentioned above we understand one thing, God works according to time and seasons and sometimes those seasons come to us disguised as challenges or problems. The wisest man who ever lived on this earth (besides Jesus) was Solomon. He talked about purpose, time and seasons. In the following verse he tells us why some unlikely people prosper and why some smart people do not. The Bible says,

> "I have observed something else under the sun. The fastest runner doesn't always win the race, and the strongest warrior doesn't always win the battle. The wise sometimes go hungry, and the skillful are not necessarily wealthy. And those who are educated don't always lead successful lives. It is all decided by chance, by being in the right place at the right time." (Ecclesiastes 9:11) (NLT)

How do we know if we are at the right place at the right time? Solomon says in the next verse, "Moreover, no man knows when his hour will come: As fish are caught in a cruel net, or birds are taken in a snare, so men are trapped by evil times that fall unexpectedly upon them." (Ecclesiastes 9:12) (NIV)

I am not saying that God inflicts us with sickness or evil to let us know about His timing. Sometimes, He will try to communicate with us only to find that we ignore Him. To get our attention He will introduce circumstances that are designed to help us refocus on Him. If we still do not respond to Him, He allows things to happen that sometimes cause pain. This speaks to our fallen nature. Pain gets our attention and focus and we will do anything to get out of pain.

We need to know for sure what originates from God and what comes from the enemy. Many people get confused about the works of God and the works of the devil. The devil comes to steal, kill and destroy. Jesus came to give us life and life more abundantly (John 10:10). The difference between the trials that God allows and what the enemy sends is the peace or the absence of peace in your heart when you are in the midst of it, and the result of the trial. When God sends a storm you will have His peace in the midst of that storm.

When God allows you to go through a trial He will give you grace and walk you through it. It may not be an easy road. That is why the Psalmist says, "Even when I walk through the darkest valley, I will not be afraid, for you are close beside me. Your rod and your staff protect and comfort me" (Psalm 23:4) (NLT). At the end you will always come out victorious and changed.

When the enemy sends a trial he is trying to steal, kill and destroy what God has given you. You will not be at peace and you will be agitated. At the end you will come out defeated and lost. How do we know *how* God disciplines us?

When God wants to deal with an area of our life He will send a person to reveal that area either through a conflict, through friendship or through His Word. Or, He will allow a circumstance to expose the area that needs to be dealt with in the light of the scriptures. The purpose is to expose the deception of the enemy by which we are blinded to certain truths from the Word of God.

Children tend to take advantage of parents who choose to coddle their kids rather than mixing their affection with authoritative discipline. Sometimes when we tell our children to do something they ignore the directive. So, as parents we say it a second time with a little more emphasis. If they still do not comply, we may raise our voices a little bit.

When children rebel and disobey their parents they need to be corrected and disciplined, even if it is painful to them at that time. As parents, we know it is for their good that we discipline our children.

The same principle applies in Christianity. God is our Father and when we ignore His instructions for a while He will correct us and discipline us for our own good. His ultimate goal is to conform us to the image, attitude, and character of His Son, Jesus Christ.

> "My son, do not despise the chastening of the Lord, Nor detest His correction; for whom the Lord loves He corrects, Just as a father the son in whom he delights." (Proverbs 3:11-12)

> "If you endure chastening, God deals with you as with sons; for what son is there whom a father does not chasten? But if you are without chastening, of which all have become partakers, then you are illegitimate and not sons." (Hebrews 12:7-8)

Some children test their parents' patience and will not respond or do something when they are first told. Others rebel against their parents and need to be disciplined. God first allows us to experience the fruit of our behavior and then He acts to chasten us if we do not heed Him.

There are three words that are used in the New Testament in relation to God's disciplinary action toward His children. God disciplines us in three stages. First, He will chasten us. If we do not heed His chastening, then He will rebuke us. If we do not listen to that rebuke, He will scourge us. Hebrews 12:5-6 says,

> "...My son, do not despise the chastening of the LORD, nor be discouraged when you are rebuked by Him; for whom the LORD loves He chastens, and scourges every son whom He receives."

The three words that are used in the above scripture are **chastening, rebuking,** and **scourging**. We see a progressive increase in the intensity of the correction. Let's look at the Greek to find what each of these words specifically means.

The word for chastening is *paideia* (Strong's G3809), which means the whole training and education of children including mind and morals; instruction which aims at increasing virtue.

> "Receive, please, instruction from His mouth, and lay up His words in your heart." (Job 22:22)

> "Listen to my instruction and be wise. Don't ignore it." (Proverbs 8:33) (NLT)

God starts with giving instruction but if we do not listen He will move to the next step and rebuke us. The word for rebuke in the Greek is *elegcho* (Strong's G1651), which means to convict; refute; or confute; generally with a suggestion of shame of the person convicted; to find fault with; correct by word; to reprehend severely; chide; admonish; reprove.

> "As many as I love, I rebuke and chasten. Therefore be zealous and repent." (Revelation 3:19)

> "O Lord, do not rebuke me in Your anger, Nor chasten me in Your hot displeasure." (Psalm 6:1)

If we still do not pay attention, God advances to the next step, which is scourging. The word used in Greek is *mastigoo* (Strong's G3146), which means to whip or flog metaphorically of God as a father chastising and training men as children by afflictions (Thayers Greek Lexicon). The Greek word *mastigoo* comes from the root word *mastix* (Strong's G3148), which means to scourge; whip; or a calamity; a misfortune sent by God to discipline or punish.

> "The Lord has chastened me severely, but He has not given me over to death." (Psalm 118:18)

Unfortunately, many of us pay attention to God only after the scourging. We will keep going until something hurts. That is not His perfect will for us. Others, because of a lack of understanding, get bitter toward God and people. One of the most difficult things to recognize is the purpose of a trial when you are in the middle of it.

Others hold on to their bitterness and grudges and this manifests as sickness and disease later in their lives. I have heard that the majority of people in hospitals with physical illnesses have sicknesses rooted in emotional causes.

What if Joseph in the Old Testament became bitter toward God or his brothers because his brothers sold him as a slave? What if He had thought, "If God really loved me He would not let me go through such things?" No, it was God taking him from one season to another until he reached the place of his destiny.

It is unfortunate that we do not hear much teaching on what to do if you get thrown into a well or cast into a prison like Paul and Silas did. If you study the lives of people who did something extraordinary, whether in the Bible or throughout history, you will see that behind every great accomplishment there is a story of great challenges.

The distance between your present life and the future you dream of is sometimes a problem. What stands between you and your Promised Land is a crisis. When you ask God for a promotion He may send a challenge. When you overcome that problem or crisis you will be promoted to the next season in your life.

The connection between Joseph and the fulfillment of his dream was the pit, persecution and the prison he endured. What promoted David to his next season in life was killing Goliath. Moses had to leave Egypt, his comfort zone, for the wilderness to enter into the next season in his life. Joshua and the Israelites had to overcome Jordan to enter the Promised Land. Shadrach, Meshach and Abed-Nego were promoted in Babylon because they went through the fire. The greater the dream, the more severe and lengthy the preparation. The greater the promotion, the hotter the fire.

In the natural realm, springtime always gives way to summer. The sun gets hotter and the temperature increases. It can be really uncomfortable to us if we live in a place where there is a lot of humidity, but that heat actually causes the trees to blossom and their fruit to grow sweeter. Without the sun's heat, plants cannot produce their fruit or food.

If you look back in your life, most breakthroughs came either in the midst of, or just after, going through a season of great trials. Just as necessity is the mother of invention; pain is often the mother of change or a new season. God works in different ways than we think or imagine.

The grape is one of the most universal of fruits and in third world countries it is one of the most expensive fruits. Most of us like to eat grapes, especially when they are sweet. How many of us realize what a grapevine has to go through to produce its fruit? Every branch needs to go through a pruning every year in order to produce the grapes. It is a painful experience but if the vine does not go through that pain, there will not be any fruit when the harvest comes.

God prunes us the same way when He takes us from one season to another so that we will bear more fruit for Him. It is not easy to go through God's pruning. You will feel like everything has come to an end. When a grapevine is pruned it looks dead. You would never think it was going to produce anything, but it is a preparation for the next season. Jesus said in John 15:1-2,

> "I am the true vine, and My Father is the vinedresser. Every branch in Me that does not bear fruit He takes away; and every branch that bears fruit He prunes, that it may bear more fruit."

One day the disciples came and asked Jesus about the signs of the end time. They wanted to know how and when to expect His return. That means they were asking Him to tell them how to recognize the beginning of that new season. Matthew 24:3 says,

> "Now as He sat on the Mount of Olives, the disciples came to Him privately, saying, "Tell us, when will these things be? And what will be the sign of Your coming, and of the end of the age?"

Jesus replied to them and said,

> "And you will hear of wars and rumors of wars. See that you are not troubled; for all these things must come to pass, but the end is not yet. For nation will rise against nation, and kingdom against kingdom. And there will be famines, pestilences, and earthquakes in various places. All these are the beginning of sorrows." (Matthew 24:6-8)

He continued to say in Matthew 24:9-10,

> "Then they will deliver you up to tribulation and kill you, and you will be hated by all nations for My name's sake. And then many will be offended, will betray one another, and will hate one another."

In other words, when you see a lot of troubles all over the world it will be a sign of the beginning of sorrows or the beginning of a new season that you will enter. Just like we go through trials and challenges before we enter into a new season in the spirit, the whole earth will go through the same to enter into its new season.

Matthew 24:21-22 says,

> "For then there will be great tribulation, such as has not been since the beginning of the world until this time, no, nor ever shall be. And unless those days were shortened, no flesh would be saved; but for the elect's sake those days will be shortened."

Jesus is clearly teaching us how to recognize the season of His second coming. Some of those signs will be great pain, death, famine, wars, pestilence, and great tribulation.

Nature itself teaches that when something gives birth there is pain involved. Pain precedes the birth of most creatures on this earth. When a new life arrives on this earth it comes as the result of pain. We give birth to new seasons in our lives as we encounter unexpected trials.

Jesus said in John 16:20-22,

> "Most assuredly, I say to you that you will weep and lament, but the world will rejoice; and you will be sorrowful, but your sorrow will be turned into joy. A woman, when she is in labor, has sorrow because her hour has come; but as soon as she has given birth to the child, she no longer remembers the anguish, for joy that a human being has been born into the world. Therefore you now have sorrow; but I will see you again and your heart will rejoice, and your joy no one will take from you."

As I am writing this book there are two major wars going on in Iraq and Afghanistan. Political unrest in countries like Pakistan, Sri Lanka, Iran, and North Korea are a growing concern. Various parts of Africa are affected by famine. Sickness like Swine Flu and other rare diseases are becoming a threat to human health.

If you study the life of Moses, after his birth he had to be separated from his mother for a short while because the king of Egypt declared that every male child who was two years and younger must be put to death. His mother hid him for three months and the time came that she could not hide him anymore.

Moses was placed in a basket and left at the shore of the river Nile, where Pharaoh's daughter came to bathe. His mother never expected to see Moses again and probably kissed him as much as she could before she put her son into that basket. It was a painful experience for both Moses and his mother.

Pharaoh's daughter took Moses to the palace and he lived there for the next forty years, until another painful experience occurred that changed Moses' life. He killed an Egyptian for the love of his people and had to flee not only from Egypt but also from any dreams of maintaining a life of significance. He might have run away from there with great disappointment and pain in the natural, but with great hope believing one day God would deliver His people from Egypt. Again, he did not know that it was the beginning of a new season in his life.

Dear child of God, do you see this pattern in God's Word again and again? That is one of the ways God communicates His timing to you. You are created for a purpose. Every purpose has a season and time. Everything works on this earth according to natural time. In the spiritual realm, everything works according to God's timing. He has timed every purpose in eternity and it manifests on this earth whenever He decides. He does not work according to our clock; months, days, or years. That is the first thing you must know about God's timing. He does not run on our schedules.

In the Old Testament we see that one of the tribes of Israel had a special ability to know God's timing.

> "The sons of Issachar who had understanding of the times, to know what Israel ought to do..." (1 Chronicles 12:32)

They informed the whole nation of Israel about what they should do in a particular season. I believe God gave them wisdom to discern the spiritual timing based on what Israel was going through as a nation at that particular time. It may have included trials, famine, calamities, lack, wars, or be based on some relationship with other nations. Or, it could have been spiritual insight God gave them.

I believe God wants to impart that same wisdom to the body of Christ worldwide. If there was ever a time that the body of Christ needed to be the light and salt of the earth; it is now. The world and its leaders are looking for answers and they are turning to ungodly counsel because they do not know where to look. God always governs history through His chosen vessels; Joseph, Moses, Joshua, Daniel, Esther, and David are some examples of how God used men and women to change the course of history.

I believe in the last days we need the wisdom of God more than ever. More than finances and anointing, it takes the wisdom of God to make a lasting impact on cultures and nations. Those individuals in the Bible who made a lasting impact on the nations they were living in accomplished this through wisdom that was given to them by God (Deut. 34:9; Psalm 105:22). Anointing and finances will be no match or substitute for God's wisdom. The Bible says in Proverbs 21:22,

> "A wise man scales the city of the mighty, and brings down the trusted stronghold."

> "For wisdom is better than rubies, and all the things one may desire cannot be compared with her." (Proverbs 8:11)

> "Wisdom is the principal thing; therefore get wisdom. And in all your getting, get understanding." (Proverbs 4:7)

Do not be discouraged or disappointed if you are going through some troubles in your life. God has not forgotten or rejected you. He is stirring up your spirit to do something great in your life. Though you may feel like God is hiding from you, surely He will come, as surely as the sun that rises every morning.

Though the dark clouds of depression and hopelessness may cover the sky above you, you can be sure of one thing; He will come. It is just a matter of time. Hold on and keep holding on and never give up. You might feel like giving up and dying a thousand times a day. No, you will not. His hand is upon you and He lovingly carved your image in the depths of His heart.

In my own life each new season began with unusual challenges. I never knew I was called to the ministry. No one told me that I would be in the ministry when I grew up. My parents did not recognize it, nor did any man of God recognize and tell me about it until I entered the ministry.

I grew up in a Christian home in India. I was an average student in school. After finishing high school I lost the interest to pursue education. It kind of discouraged my parents and they tried their best to get me back to school again, but I fooled them and went to movies and other places when they sent me to study.

I was discouraged, depressed and I did not know what to do. I wanted to study but I could not because I did not have the ability to grasp anything. I did not know my purpose and I did not know English either. I used to read my Bible and cry before God, asking Him to reveal the purpose of my life. That pain was a sign of the beginning of a new season in my life.

One day I had this desire in my heart to go to a Bible College. I wanted to get away from my father and my home. Little did I know that it was God who put that desire in my heart. I asked my father to send me to Bible College but he would not let me go. He wanted me to study and become a medical doctor.

He was not against me going to Bible College. He wanted to make sure that I was called and he was concerned about who was going to support me and how I would make a living. I believe those were the concerns he had in his heart. Finally, I cried and asked him and hesitantly he granted me the permission to go to a Bible College.

When I was eighteen, I started this journey by boarding a train and traveling for three days to reach New Delhi, the capital city of India. From that point on, God's hand was evident in my life.

Suddenly, my understanding was opened and I had a desire to study. Within three months, I began to speak and preach in English. I could memorize five to ten pages of notes within a short period of time and I became the number one student academically in most of my subjects. In my final year, the faculty elected me to be the leader of the student body. We had about five hundred students from eighteen different language groups.

It is amazing to see what God has done in a short period of time. We are preaching the gospel to one of the largest unreached people groups in the world. One among every five persons worldwide is an Indian. We helped plant 80 churches and trained more than 7,000 pastors and leaders. We take care of orphans and destitute children. All things are possible with those who believe. What happened in your life is nothing compared to what God has in store for you. Get ready to enter into a new season of your life with God!

In the next chapter we are going to see how different people in the Bible recognized God's timing for their life when they went through adverse circumstances. They entered into new seasons of their lives in the midst of their adversities.

Chapter 5

INDIVIDUALS AND GOD'S TIMING

"My times are in Your hand;
Deliver me from the hand of my enemies,
And from those who persecute me." Psalm 31:15

GOD HAS A SPECIFIC TIMING FOR EVERYTHING THAT PERTAINS TO OUR LIFE ON THIS EARTH. As I mentioned in the second chapter, our lives grow in different stages and seasons. When we pass one stage we cannot go back to that stage again. When a person is grown up he cannot return to his childhood. We cannot go back to first grade again in school. In the spirit, God has timed our lives as to when things should happen on this earth.`

Each individual person has a specific timing for his or her purpose on this earth, but it is not limited to any age or place. God is a God of mercy and longsuffering. If we miss one season, He will give us another chance and then another chance. It is not as if you miss an appointment for an interview and you lose your chance.

In the spirit, if you miss an appointment God will give you another one. God will open another door and the sun will rise again on your horizon. I have found that God will take our mistakes and failures and turn them for our benefit and His glory. It is difficult to see this when you are going through something. But, if you look back in your life you will see how God has orchestrated each incident and how His purpose played out in all things for our good.

The Bible says in Ecclesiastes 3:1-2

> "To everything there is a season, a time for every purpose under heaven: A time to be born, and a time to die; a time to plant, and a time to pluck what is planted."

We are not roaming this earth without a purpose. God has brought each of us to this earth for a specific purpose and for a specific period of time. Jesus was born in the fullness of time and the time of His death was appointed by God. No one could touch or take His life before that time. So, too, each of us was sent to this earth as the Father sent Jesus. We have a specific mission and lifespan decided by God. We read in John 7:30, "Therefore they sought to take Him; but no one laid a hand on Him, because His hour had not yet come."

As long as you are walking in God's purpose; no one can touch your life or harm you. Jesus is the best example of this because, from the beginning of His ministry, many wanted to kill Him but could not because His time had not yet come.

John 8:20 says,

> "These words Jesus spoke in the treasury, as He taught in the temple; and no one laid hands on Him, for His hour had not yet come."

A few days later, Jesus said His hour had come. He knew God's timing for

His life very well.

John 12:23 says,

> "But Jesus answered them, saying, "The hour has come that the Son of Man should be glorified."

John 13:1 reads,

> "Now before the Feast of the Passover, when Jesus knew that His hour had come that He should depart from this world to the Father..."

That is the way we should live our lives. Paul and Peter sensed the imminence of their departures from this world (2 Timothy 4:6; 2 Peter 1:14).

Each individual is different and unique, so you cannot compare yourself with others or copy their lives. No, it would be a huge mistake. God's purpose for you, and how He will deal with you, is different from anyone else on this earth. We do not see in the Bible God using any two people the same way. There is only one burning bush and one Red Sea parting. We can learn from their experiences the principles and precepts God uses to communicate His timing.

We are going to examine some individuals from the Bible to see how they experienced pain, struggles, discouragement, and rejection before they entered into a new season in their walk with the Lord.

ABRAHAM

Abraham was called by God and was given great promises to be a blessing to the whole world. It is interesting to see how God developed his character and patience through the things he endured in his life. Many people want the promises of God, but they do not understand that they need to endure great pain in order to inherit those promises. Faith alone is not enough to inherit the promises; it needs to be mixed with patience.

> "That you do not become sluggish, but imitate those who through faith and patience inherit the promises." (Hebrews 6:12)

Patience is not easily developed in our lives. It is only developed when we yield our lives to the sufferings that we experience (James 1:2-4).

Abram started his journey from Haran when he was seventy-five years old. The Bible says he reached Canaan and kept moving toward the south. After a while, there arose a great challenge in his life. There was a famine in the land and he had to look for food and water, so Abram decided to go to Egypt. I believe this was the beginning of a new season.

Abram did not ask God whether or not he should go to Egypt. It is very important that you do not make choices based on your emotions when you face challenges in life. We need to wait and hear from God before we make a move.

When he was in Egypt, the people saw that Abram's wife was very beautiful and Pharaoh, the king of Egypt, took Abram's wife, Sarai, to his palace. I believe that was a sleepless night for him; wondering what would happen to his wife. God protected her by plaguing Pharaoh and his household. He restored Sarai to Abram and they had to leave Egypt. It was God's plan for them to move out of Egypt. God did not want them to stay in Egypt.

Then Abram went to Bethel and pitched his tent there. There he encountered another problem in his life. There arose strife between his servants and Lot's servants. There was no peace in the family. There was tension and strained relationship. Abram called Lot and told him they could not have such strife so they would have to separate.

After Lot was separated, the Lord appeared to Abram and reassured him of the promises. And, again, he moved from Bethel to Hebron. It seems like whenever Abram received a Word from God he would move to a new location. Every new season comes with a new revelation or new promise from God.

In Genesis 15:1, we read that the Word of the Lord came to him in a vision and said,

> "Do not be afraid, Abram. I am your shield, your exceedingly great reward."

Abram was not encouraged by hearing that. He wondered what the use was of this shield and reward if he did not have any children. The following verse reveals his frustration.

> "But Abram said, "Lord God, what can you give me? I have
> no son, so my slave Eliezer from Damascus will get everything
> I own after I die." Abram said, "Look, you have given me no
> son, so a slave born in my house will inherit everything I have."
> (Genesis 15:2-3) (NCV)

That was the beginning of a new season Abram was about to enter. God asked him to bring the sacrifice and at the end of the sacrifice the Bible says, "On the same day the LORD made a covenant with Abram." (Genesis 15:18)

During this time, because they did not yet have any children, Sarai came up with an idea to help God fulfill his promise. She gave Abram her maid, Hagar, and she bore him a child named Ishmael. Abram stepped out of God's timing for his life and brought forth Ishmael. It was not God's will for Abram and Sarai to have Ishmael by Hagar (Genesis 16:1-4). They thought they were helping God to fulfill His promise. If He needed it, surely He would have asked them. I believe the enemy has deceived more saints in this regard than any other matter in life. He pushes them to step out of God's timing and bring forth wrong results at the wrong time.

King Saul failed in the same matter with Samuel. Samuel told him to wait for him to come to offer the sacrifice but he did not come at the time Saul expected. Saul became impatient and offered the sacrifice, and then Samuel immediately showed up. The king gave in to the pressure and fear of men and disobeyed God by doing the wrong thing at the right time.

It was too late for Saul. He lost the kingdom, the anointing, and all of his family (1 Samuel 13:10-14). I pray that God will give us patience to wait for His timing even if it is not convenient for us. It is worth the wait when you are waiting on God. The Bible says those who wait upon the Lord shall never be ashamed (Psalm 34:5).

The next season started in Abram's life when he was ninety-nine years old. The Lord came and talked to him about his children and made a new covenant with him. He changed his name to Abraham, father of a multitude (Genesis 17:5). As a sign of the covenant, God instituted circumcision for all men (Genesis 17:9-10).

In chapter twenty of Genesis, we see Abraham facing another challenge with Abimelech because he also took Sarah from Abraham. God intervened again and protected Sarah and she was restored. But this time when she was restored, Abimelech gave many material blessings to Abraham (Genesis 20:14).

One year later, the Lord fulfilled His promise and gave Abraham and Sarah a son and they named him Isaac. After this, Abraham had to pass a final test before he became what God had promised to make him.

One day God told him to offer his son Isaac as a sacrifice. Abraham may have gone through the greatest mental struggle when he heard that. But, he obeyed God, regardless of his emotional pain. He took Isaac and went to Mount Moriah and prepared everything to offer his son as a burnt offering. The Angel of the Lord appeared to him and told him not to kill his son and instead provided a ram for the offering.

After this the Angel of the LORD called him and established the covenantal promise to him forever.

Genesis 22:15-18 says,

> "Then the Angel of the LORD called to Abraham a second time out of heaven, and said: "By myself I have sworn, says the LORD, because you have done this thing, and have not withheld your son, your only son – blessing I will bless you, and multiplying I will multiply your descendants as the stars of the heaven and as the sand which is on the seashore; and your descendants shall possess the gate of their enemies. In your seed all the nations of the earth shall be blessed, because you have obeyed My voice."

I believe there was great struggle in Abraham's family when God asked him to offer Isaac as a sacrifice. You can only imagine the pain of a mother who bore a child at her old age and now has to give it up. It is interesting to see after this incident that Abraham did not go back to Sarah but stayed in Beersheba (Genesis 22:19), while Sarah was in Hebron. When Sarah died in Hebron, Abraham came there to mourn for her (Genesis 23:1-2).

Joseph

I do not believe anyone else went through as much pain and adverse circumstances as Joseph. We know that it was all for a purpose, and that God was behind all that he had experienced. We are going to look in detail at each incident and how it helped him to go from one season to another.

Joseph was the eleventh son of Jacob and was loved by his father very much. He was feeding the sheep with his older brothers and he brought ill reports about them to his father. From that we can see he was a man of integrity; faithful to the task given to him and his father loved him. For this reason, his brothers hated him and could not talk to him peaceably. Genesis 37:4 says,

> "And when his brethren saw that their father loved him more than all his brethren, they hated him, and could not speak peaceably unto him." (KJV)

This was not an easy time for Joseph. Imagine living in a house where ten of your brothers do not like you and would not talk to you in peace. This was the first recorded challenge Joseph faced. As I said earlier, stress and strained relationships could be signs of the beginning of a new season in the spirit.

Joseph did not treat his brothers the way they treated him. The next verse says he had a dream from God. He shared his dream with his brothers and they hated him more.

> "And Joseph dreamed a dream, and he told it to his brethren: and they hated him yet the more." (Genesis 37:5) (KJV)

He had another dream and shared that with his father and brethren. His father rebuked him but kept the dream in his heart. The Bible says his brethren envied him. This is the first stage of fulfilling your purpose. God will put a dream, a vision, or a burning desire in your heart. Then He will train you and prepare you to fulfill that dream.

> "And his brethren envied him; but his father observed the saying." (Genesis 37:11) (KJV)

Joseph was ready to enter into his next season. Before they hated him, and now; one degree further, they envied him. He passed that test and was sent to find his brothers in the field. When his brothers saw him they decided to kill him, but because of the intervention of Reuben, they did not kill him. Instead, they put him in a pit (Genesis 37:18-25). They cast him into the pit and rejected him.

We do not see in any of these incidents Joseph reacting to them in any ungodly manner. He endured their rejection and kept moving into his next season while his brothers did not. I thought, "How can this be Joseph's new season?" His situation was going from bad to worse. First, they hated him, and then envied him, and now they wanted to kill him.

Well, in the spirit he was making progress though in the natural, situations were not changed. In his spirit man he was making super advancements by enduring the hardship and not reacting in the flesh. That is what God wants from all of us. Just like when you plant a seed, you will not see any visible changes or outward growth for a few days, but there are great changes taking place inside that seed. It grows downward first and then it is just a matter of time before the growth spurt occurs.

Before our promotion manifests in the natural, God works in our hearts to build character. When we look on the outside it seems we have made no progress. Things may not have changed a bit, but look inside your heart and you will see God busily shaping it. Next, He will help you put the roots of your character down so that it can sustain your life when you grow outward and upward.

The seed grows downward first before it springs up on the surface of the ground. It seemed Joseph was going downward, but in the spirit he was going upward from one season to the other. There is only progress in the spirit and there is no regress.

You might go from crisis to crisis and feel like your situation is going from bad to worse. If it is God ordained, (if you are saved and walking in obedience it is God ordained), the end result will be a big impact. Joseph was going from one crisis to another. His character was being formed for the powerful destiny he had in his life. The greater the purpose; the greater the trials you will have. The greater the anointing; the greater the test you need to go through. The greater the position; the longer the wait, hatred, and envy you will face.

> "Then they took him, and cast him into a pit..." (Genesis 37:24)

We know it was not easy for Joseph to go through these experiences. He was a human being and felt the pain, disappointment, discomfort, agony, and emotional struggles in his life.

His brothers saw the merchants of the Ishmaelites coming and they decided to sell him to them for twenty pieces of silver.

> "...the brothers pulled Joseph up and lifted him out of the pit, and sold Joseph to the Ishmaelites for twenty shekles of silver. And they took Joseph to Egypt." (Genesis 37:28)

Now he was sold as a slave and totally abandoned by his brothers! He did not get a chance to see his father or say goodbye to anyone. It was a heartbreaking experience for Joseph, but he was enduring it with great patience and love. That is the key to overcoming the trials of life. As long as we react in the flesh we will not enter into our new season.

We need to finish our current season before God will let us enter into our new season. When God sees that His love is displayed in our lives even in the midst of our pain; we are qualified for a promotion. In essence, each season is a test to show whether or not we are able to give God's love to the people who persecute us.

Imagine you were brought as a slave to the place of your destiny! What could look more bleak and hopeless than that? God works in ways that we cannot fathom in the natural. You might ask, "How can I be a slave in a place where I am supposed to be the prince?"

Sometimes we see God's hand only in the positive incidents in life. One of the reasons we fail to recognize God's timing is because we fail to see God's hand in our negative and adverse circumstances. This usually causes great emotional pain, but precedes spiritual promotion. Opportunities often come to us disguised as adversities.

The Bible says,

> "Moreover He (God) called for a famine in the land; He

(God) destroyed all the provision of bread. He sent a man before them—Joseph—who was sold as a slave. They hurt his
feet with fetters, He was laid in irons. Until the time that his
word came to pass, the word of the Lord tested him." (Psalm
105:16-19)

God was setting the stage by bringing the famine to fulfill the destiny of
Joseph. If there was not a famine he would not have reached the palace of
Pharaoh. Why God chose the famine, we do not know. It is very unfor-
tunate that some "faith teachers" and their followers do not believe that
God will cause such things to happen in our lives.

Joseph entered his new season after he was sold to the Ishmaelites and they
sold him to Potiphar the captain of Pharaoh's guard.

"And the Midianites sold him into Egypt unto Potiphar, an of-
ficer of Pharaoh, and captain of the guard." (Genesis 37:36)

Joseph prospered in Egypt because the Lord was with him. His master
made him lord of all his substance and the Lord prospered Potiphar because of Joseph.

The time came for Joseph to enter into a new season. Potiphar's wife asked
him to lie with her. Joseph refused many times but the woman kept per-
sisting and finally caught him by his garments. He ran away, leaving his
garment, and did not commit adultery with her (Genesis 39:7-13).

The woman deceived other people by lying to them about Joseph and also
told her husband that it was Joseph who tried to lay with her. His master
was very angry at Joseph and put him in the prison where king's prisoners
were kept.

"Then Joseph's master took him and put him into the prison,
a place where the king's prisoners were confined. And he was
there in the prison." (Genesis 39:20)

Again, we see that before Joseph entered into his new season he went
through a painful experience. Imagine that you are going through pain for
things you did not do, or put in a prison for a crime you did not commit.
Have you ever been falsely accused of something that you did not do by

someone in authority and punished for it? God had a purpose behind that and He was getting ready to do something new in your life. That is one of the ways God works and communicates His timing to us.

In all these Joseph did not try to prove himself or defend himself. He committed his life to God who judges righteously and vindicates at the right time. We see the same attitude in Jesus' life when he was punished for the crimes He did not commit (1 Peter 2:23). That is the attitude God wants from all of us and we will go through trials until we reach that place.

It does not make any sense in our natural thinking that God would let us go through trials to accomplish His will in our lives. Is God not a loving father? Then, why would He let His children suffer? This is a question that has been asked by millions of saints for centuries.

Over the years, I've learned something about the human heart (the fallen nature). It will change only when we go through pain. As I said earlier, pain is the mother of change. Also, the Bible says that God will not allow us to go through temptation more than we can bear, but with the temptation He makes a way out.

> "No temptation has overtaken you except such as is common to man; but God is faithful, who will not allow you to be tempted beyond what you are able, but with the temptation will also make the way of escape, that you may be able to bear it." (1 Corinthians 10:13)

During this time, Pharaoh's chief butler and baker offended him and they, too, were cast into the king's prison. The Bible says they stayed there for a season.

> "And the captain of the guard charged Joseph with them, and he ministered unto them: and they continued a season in ward." (Genesis 40:4) (ASV)

The next season Joseph spent in the prison with the king's prisoners, mostly those who used to work in the palace (Genesis 39:20). I believe Joseph spent a lot of time with these people and might have asked a lot of questions about the king, the palace, and how things worked in Egypt. If it were me, I would have asked and tried to learn everything I could about how the king conducted his business. It was a learning experience for Joseph that prepared him for the next season. Each season is a learning experience for the next.

This was the final test in Joseph's life before he was appointed to the position and purpose for which he was born. You see in his life that each season brought new relationships and connections that he needed. First, it was his brothers, and then he was sold to the Ishmaelites. Next, it was Potiphar, then the keeper of the prison, and then it was the butler and the baker in the prison. I deal with relationships and God's timing in detail in a different chapter.

One day the butler and the baker each had a dream that was troubling. Joseph interpreted their dreams and the butler was re-appointed, but the baker was hanged just like Joseph predicted. Joseph tried to get help through the butler but he forgot about him (Genesis 40:5-23).

After two years, Pharaoh had a dream that no one in Egypt could interpret. The chief butler then remembered Joseph and told Pharaoh about him. He was brought to the king and he interpreted his dream. The interpretation pleased the king and he appointed Joseph second in command in all of Egypt (Genesis 41).

MOSES

Through Joseph God brought the Israelites to Egypt. God prospered them and they became a great multitude. When the time came for them to go back to the land that God promised their fathers, God sent Moses to deliver them. The Bible says God caused the Egyptians to hate His people.

Psalm 105:23-26 says,

> "Israel also came into Egypt, and Jacob dwelt in the land of Ham. He increased His people greatly, and made them stronger than their enemies. He turned their heart to hate His people, to deal craftily with His servants. He sent Moses His servant, and Aaron whom He had chosen."

Moses is one of my favorite characters in the Bible because of the relationship he had with God. It was not an easy road for Moses to reach such a relationship with God. He was born into such adverse circumstances that he was sentenced to death even before he was born. There was nothing for Moses to look forward to in the natural, only death was waiting for him. Let's look at the story of Moses in the King James Bible.

> "And he (Pharaoh) said, When ye do the office of a midwife to the Hebrew women, and see them upon the stools; if it be a son, then ye shall kill him: but if it be a daughter, she shall live." (Exodus 1:16)

But God had a different purpose and He always overrides the plan and verdict of man. He had a destiny for Moses that no man could destroy. When he was born, Moses' mother saw that he was a goodly child and she hid him for three months. After three months she could not hide him any longer. She made a basket, then put him in it and laid it by the river bank.

Here Moses is getting ready to enter into his new season. His mother may have thought that she would not see him again. She might have cried all day after leaving him at the river bank. It was a painful experience for both of them. Moses would have felt terrified in that basket.

Pharaoh's daughter came to wash herself in the river and her maids found the basket and brought it to her. She saw that it was a Hebrew child and felt compassion on him. His sister was watching all this and she approached Pharaoh's daughter and asked her if she wanted a woman to nurse the child. She gave her permission and his sister went and brought his mother.

Pharaoh's daughter told her to take the baby and nurse him until he was weaned and bring him back to the palace afterward. This is totally a miracle. Not only did his mother get to nurse him, but she got paid for doing it!

> "And Pharaoh's daughter said unto her, Take this child away, and nurse it for me, and I will give thee thy wages. And the woman took the child and nursed it." (Exodus 2:9) (KJV)

After he was weaned, the boy's mother brought him to the palace and he became Pharaoh's grandson. Pharaoh's daughter called his name Moses because she drew him out of the water. This was the beginning of the next season in Moses' life. He was separated from his family and adopted by Pharaoh's daughter. Naturally, it would have been a painful experience for both Moses and his family.

He grew up in the palace and learned all of the wisdom and arts of Egypt. During this time, Moses somehow came to know that he was not an Egyptian but an Israelite. Though the Bible is not clear about how Moses recognized that he was a Hebrew, He began to recognize his destiny. As the Bible says, God has written eternity in our hearts (Ecclesiastes 3:11).

One day he went out to see his people and saw how terribly they were treated by Pharaoh and his men and he saw an Egyptian smiting a Hebrew. Moses killed the Egyptian and buried him in the sand (Exodus 2:11-12). The next day he saw two Hebrews fighting each other and he offered to settle the issue, but they rejected him and reminded him of the murder he had committed.

It brought such feelings of guilt and fear to Moses that he fled Egypt and went to Midian. Leaving Egypt was the end of another season in his life and the time had come for the next season to begin.

In Midian, Moses found his wife and shepherded his father-in-law's sheep for the next forty years. Moses entered a couple of new seasons during this time. One was when he got married and the next was learning how to feed and take care of sheep. God was preparing him for the task that lay ahead.

Moses may have gone through all kinds of depression and discouragement during this time because he grew up as a prince and was now feeding someone else's sheep. It was really a very humbling experience for Moses. One day he took the sheep to Horeb, the mountain of God.

The Angel of the LORD appeared to Moses in a flame of fire out of the midst of a bush, and him looked and saw the bush burned with fire but not consumed. That was the beginning of another new season in his life. It was God's timing for him to begin to walk in his destiny.

God commissioned him to go to Egypt to deliver His people. Through a series of miracles and judgments, God brought the people out of Egypt.

Very quickly he went from feeding sheep to leading six hundred thousand men, plus women and children. He entered his next season when he brought the people out of Egypt. He had to go through several hardships and temptations in the wilderness. Because the people were not like sheep, they rebelled and murmured against Moses and God.

DAVID

David is a type of Christ in the Old Testament. His life gives us more spiritual and moral truth than any other character in the Bible. In his life we see that with each new season he changed his location. He was originally from Bethlehem and was the youngest son of Jesse.

> "Now David was the son of that Ephrathite of Bethlehem Judah, whose name was Jesse, and who had eight sons." (1 Samuel 17:12)

The first season of David's life began in Bethlehem, feeding his father's sheep. King Saul disobeyed God so He sent Samuel to David's house to anoint him as the new King of Israel. Samuel anointed David but he did not immediately become a king. That was just the beginning of his next season.

One day his father sent him with some gifts for his brothers who were in the army of King Saul. When he reached the battlefield, he heard about Goliath and the challenge Israel was facing. David agreed to fight the giant. God gave him victory and he killed Goliath. This pleased King Saul and he was brought in front of the king.

The women of Israel came out to celebrate the victory and they began singing and dancing, praising David more than they praised the king. This displeased Saul and he began to feel jealousy toward David. Saul then began to be tormented by an evil spirit and they brought David to Gibeah to King Saul's palace, to play the harp for him.

David stayed in the palace for a while and Saul envied David more and more; he even tried to kill him. David may have thought that his life was going to end there and lost all hope. No, it was just the beginning of a painful season for him. David had to flee for his life.

"So David fled and escaped, and went to Samuel at Ramah, and told him all that Saul had done to him. And he and Samuel went and stayed in Naioth." (1 Samuel 19:18)

From then on David fled from one place to another in a race for his life. It may have been one of the longest and most painful seasons faced by anyone recorded in the Bible. However, it was the preparation for the next season God had for him.

This is where many people make mistakes in their lives. Just because you are anointed does not mean it is God's time for you to function in that anointing or in that office. If we do not recognize God's timing, we can lose the anointing and our purpose. Many people step out of God's timing and start businesses or ministries that wreck their lives. Then they turn away from God and get bitter toward Him.

The way God works is this: He will put a completed picture of your destiny in your heart but may not tell you the details about how to get there. The details and specific guidance come when you daily listen to the voice of the Holy Spirit and follow His leading.

The feeling to step out and do things will be so strong but you need to restrain yourself and surrender your dreams to God daily. Just because God put a picture of your destiny in your heart does not mean it will begin to manifest the next day. The fulfillment of your dream could be many years down the road.

What if David had rebelled against Saul and tried to be the king before his time or season had arrived? That would have been the biggest mistake of his life. David had an understanding about God's timing. I believe he received that both from the Holy Spirit and from his association with Samuel. Samuel may have advised him about God's way of doing things. David was anointed and chosen by God but his time had not yet arrived.

I have seen many people get into positions in ministry and in business before their time through manipulation and fleshly influence, and later regret it and be faced with great troubles. May the Lord keep us all from such traps and give us wisdom and patience to wait for His timing. There is nothing worse than being appointed to a position before our time. If it happens we will destroy ourselves and cause great damage to other people.

It was not an easy season for David. Many times he did not know whether he would make it. But, it was a preparation for his new season as one of the greatest kings in history. Every new season is preceded by a great time of testing and trials. Do not be discouraged and lose heart if you are going through a great time of testing and trials. You are being prepared for your next promotion and must endure whatever comes your way. It may not seem enjoyable because no testing seems enjoyable when you go through it.

Hebrews 12:11 says,

> "Now no chastening seems to be joyful for the present, but painful; nevertheless, afterward it yields the peaceable fruit of righteousness to those who have been trained by it."

Studying the lives of those whom God used is the best way to encourage ourselves when we are going through such seasons.

After the death of King Saul, God spoke to David to go to Hebron, one of the cities of Judah. There the men anointed David to be the King of Judah. That was the beginning of his next season.

> "And David brought up the men who were with him, every man with his household. So they dwelt in the cities of Hebron. Then the men of Judah came, and there they anointed David king over the house of Judah." (2 Samuel 2:3-4)

David was king over the house of Judah for seven and a half years. This anointing also marked the start of a fight between David and the house of Saul. "Now there was a long war between the house of Saul and the house of David. But David grew stronger, and the house of Saul grew weaker and weaker." (2 Samuel 3:1)

After seven and a half years, all the elders of Israel came and anointed him to be the king over Israel (2 Samuel 5:3). He ruled Israel for thirty-three years and he was blessed in every way. He never lost a battle and God gave him victory wherever he went (2 Samuel 8:6, 14).

We see from David's life the fruit of moving in God's timing, but also what happens when we do not move according to God's timing. We read in 2 Samuel 11:1,

> "It happened in the spring of the year, at the time when kings go out to battle, that David sent Joab and his servants with him, and all Israel; and they destroyed the people of Ammon and besieged Rabbah. But David remained at Jerusalem."

David became complacent from all the victories God had given him in his life. Maybe he was tired of war. We do not know the exact reason, but he did not go out to battle when he was supposed to go. The scripture specifically says, "When *kings* go out to battle," but David remained in Jerusalem in his palace. He was at the right place at the wrong time. He was supposed to be out there fighting.

One evening he arose from his bed and walked on the roof of his house and, looking in the wrong direction, saw the wrong thing. That is what happens when we are at the right place at the wrong time. We will see stuff we should not see and get into things we are not supposed to get into. David was carried away by his emotions after seeing a woman taking a bath. He desired her in his heart and brought her into his house and slept with her.

Then he tried to hide the matter, but the sin was compounded when he found out that the woman became pregnant. Eventually, he plotted against her husband, killed him and took her as his wife. I believe it was the most painful experience David might have gone through in his life. It not only marred his testimony, but also opened doors to lots of trouble in his life and family. What a price to pay when we are out of our season and time. We learn a valuable lesson from his life about following our time and seasons. The Bible says in 2 Samuel 11:27,

> "...But the thing that David had done displeased the LORD."

Many times, we step out of God's timing and bring forth spiritual offspring that displeases the Lord. It could be a ministry project, starting a new venture, business, relationship, or anything that is out of step with God. It opens doors for the enemy to come in and introduce all kinds of havoc in our lives. And, if the problem is big enough, it can destroy our very existence. Many have lost their families or God's call on their lives, and caused great damage to the body of Christ bringing reproach to the Lord's name. We read in 2 Samuel 12:13-14,

> "So David said to Nathan, "I have sinned against the LORD." And Nathan said to David, "The LORD also has put away your sin; you shall not die. However, because by this deed *you have given great occasion to the enemies of the LORD to blaspheme*, the child also who is born to you shall surely die." (Italics added)

I have stepped out of God's timing in my life by starting ministry projects and programs, and have paid a great price to continue or shut them down. Just because God has given you a desire in your heart to do something does not mean it is His time to do it. Wait until He says, "NOW!"

Later in David's life we see that he had a desire to build a temple but God spoke to him and said his son, not David, was supposed to build it. He obeyed God this time and made all the preparations for the building of the temple.

PAUL

Paul was one of the religious leaders of his time and was a Pharisee. He was well educated in Old Testament theology and was very zealous for God. Before he met Jesus he was destroying the churches and persecuting the believers.

> "As for Saul, he made havoc of the church, entering every house, and dragging off men and women, committing them to prison." (Acts 8:3)

> "Then Saul, still breathing threats and murder against the disciples of the Lord, went to the high priest and asked letters from him to the synagogues of Damascus, so that if he found any who were of the Way, whether men or women, he might bring them bound to Jerusalem." (Acts 9:1-2)

Jesus appeared to Paul, then called Saul, on the way to Damascus. God struck him down to the ground and Saul became blind. Imagine how helpless and embarrassed he would have felt. When he got up from the ground, he could not see anything so others led him by the hand. It was a painful experience for Saul. He remained blind for the next three days until a disciple called Ananias laid his hands on him to regain his eye sight.

Those three days were the most dramatic days of Saul's life. So many things took place in him at once. He was so totally changed from one direction to the other that it was unbelievable. He had to change the way he thought, he had to change the mission of his life, and he had to change the way he worshiped God.

He had to change what he was preaching and he had to change what he believed up to that point. It was a revolutionary experience. Paul entered a new season in his life through that extraordinary encounter and stepped into the destiny God had for him.

Jesus spoke to him in the vision and he was called into the ministry. He was baptized and got filled with the Holy Spirit. It was a very dramatic beginning of a new season. The very thing he hated to preach and do; God called him to preach and made him an apostle. I believe he did not recognize his spiritual timing, so God had to knock him on the ground and kind of forcefully bring the revelation to him.

He began to preach the gospel right away in Damascus, but the Jews did not receive him and tried to kill him. He escaped through a basket and I believe he went to Arabia where he spent the next three years. That was the beginning of another new season in his life. He did not start his miraculous ministry right after his conversion. It was after many years. Some theologians say it may have taken fifteen years to begin the ministry God called him to.

He was a member of the church in Antioch, serving the church and the leaders. We see in the book of Acts that when the church in Antioch took an offering for the church in Judea, they sent it with Paul and Barnabas (Acts 11:29-30).

In Acts, chapter 13, we read that as the church in Antioch was praying and fasting, the Holy Spirit spoke to them to separate Barnabas and Saul for the ministry He had called them to. The leaders of the church prayed and laid hands on them; then sent them out.

Thus, Paul began his missionary journeys through which he established most of the churches he started. He had three missionary journeys. God used him mightily and the gospel was spread throughout the known world. We see in Paul's life that each new season began with a challenge or painful experience. In each season, he had a new relationship and a new location.

There are three levels of walking with the Lord after you are born again. Most Christians come to the Lord because they experienced His power or blessing in their lives. That is the first level, where you seek God for material blessings or favor. The second level is when you seek God for His power or for His anointing. But, you should not stay at that level. What will you feel if your children come to you only when they need something? Eventually, you will feel sad or hurt. God is our heavenly Father and He feels the same.

Please do not seek God for His power or blessings. You need to pass that season and enter into the third level, where you seek Him because you want to know Him and enjoy being with Him; not for any benefits. Spend time to be with Him and walk with Him daily, and He will meet all your needs.

MISSING GOD'S TIMING

Paul was not a person who always walked in God's will and timing. Sometimes leaders can go off track by assuming they are doing the right thing. We see one such incident in Paul's life. He was a Jew and always had a passion to reach the Jews with the gospel.

The Jews were not willing to give up their tradition and law and accept the salvation and righteousness that comes through faith in Jesus. Paul began his ministry among the Jews and it soon turned very sour. He had to leave the Jews and go to the Gentiles.

He was an apostle called to reach the Gentiles, but he was not willing to give up the zeal to reach his own people. Though He had extraordinary success among the Gentiles and planted many churches, he kept striving to go to the apostles in Jerusalem to witness about his ministry.

There is not clear evidence in the Bible of Jesus telling Paul to keep going back to Jerusalem to share with the church there about what God was doing among the Gentiles. One such incident is mentioned in the book of Acts chapter 19:21, "When these things were accomplished, Paul purposed in the Spirit, when he had passed through Macedonia and Achaia, to go to Jerusalem, saying, "After I have been there, I must also see Rome."

Wherever he went after that, the Holy Spirit told him not to go to Jerusalem. But he was determined to go and did not heed the warnings.

Acts 20:22-23 says,

> "And see, now I go bound in the spirit to Jerusalem, not knowing the things that will happen to me there, except that the Holy Spirit testifies in every city, saying that chains and tribulations await me."

There was a particular incident in chapter 21 where, by the Holy Spirit, he was told not to go to Jerusalem again.

Acts 21:4 reads,

> "And finding disciples, we stayed there seven days. They told Paul through the Spirit not to go up to Jerusalem."

He went to Jerusalem and the brethren received him, but they asked him to join the people who were observing Jewish customs according to the Law. He listened to them and compromised the Gospel of Grace he was preaching.

He went there with the purpose of testifying to them of the Gospel of Grace (Acts 20:24). Against his wishes, he compromised because of fear and faced much persecution by the people (Acts 21:17-36).

This is the same Paul who once rebuked Peter for showing a double standard between the Gentile and Jewish believers. When the Jewish leaders were not around, Peter would eat with the Gentile believers. When a Jewish leader or apostle was around, Peter would separate from the Gentiles and act like a Jew (Galatians 2:11-14).

Paul did the same thing in his life. I believe he missed God's timing in going to Jerusalem and went there by his own decision. Lord, please give us the wisdom and humility to wait for your timing and listen to Your Spirit no matter where we are in life. Amen.

ALL THINGS WORK TOGETHER FOR OUR GOOD

Our God is a God who brings honey from the rock and sweetness from bitter experiences.

> "He made him draw honey from the rock, and oil from the flinty rock." (Deuteronomy 32:13)

> "...And with honey from the rock I would have satisfied you." (Psalm 81:16)

You will be faced with situations similar to rocks but, at the end, from the same rock He will give you honey. This means that He will turn that situation into something that is sweet. What was pain in your last season will become your passion in the new season. You will be able to identify with fellow believers who are going through similar experiences and feel the passion and have the wisdom to help them.

Once you are saved, your circumstances are in God's hands. Once you commit your life to God and receive Christ into your life, you do not belong to yourself. You belong to God and no one can pluck you out of God's hands.

> "My sheep hear My voice, and I know them, and they follow Me. And I give them eternal life, and they shall never perish; neither shall anyone snatch them out of My hand. My Father, who has given them to Me, is greater than all; and no one is able to snatch them out of My Father's hand." (John 10:27-29)

I want to share with you that from the moment you gave your life to Christ you belong to Him and the Holy Spirit will begin to perfect you and transform you into the image of Christ. This is largely accomplished through the hardships and trials we encounter in our daily lives.

Every new season brings a higher revelation of God into your life. With every new revelation comes a new blessing. Every new season also brings a new level of testing, and every new season requires a higher level or a new dimension of faith in your life. In the Kingdom, trials are not the end of your life but the sign of new beginnings. In the spirit, trials are not hindrances to blessings; trials precede every blessing.

Many years ago, after graduating from the Bible College in India, I was working in North India with an evangelistic team. You may not know much about the Northern part of India. It is considered one of the least evangelized areas on this earth. It is one of the toughest areas in which to preach the gospel.

While I was in Uttar Pradesh, one of the states in North India and the cradle of the Hindu religion, one evening I got a call from my brother to come home. My mother had been ill and was taken to the hospital. I traveled back to my state and went to the hospital to see my mother. She was in a very serious condition and we went from one hospital to another but her situation did not improve.

Finally, we decided to bring her home and put our trust in God for her healing. We brought her home and she was bedridden for almost a month. Early one morning she left her earthly home and went to be with the Lord. Afterward, I felt lost. I was in great pain. I did not feel that I should go back to the same organization so I joined another organization for short-term training. That was the beginning of a new season in my life. That decision opened many doors and eventually I was able to come to the US for higher study.

Now I am beginning to recognize that in the spirit every painful trial is the end of one season and a sign of the birth of a new season. You can be sure of one thing, if you love God in your heart and your desire is only to do His will, at the end everything works out for your good.

> "And we know that all things work together for good to those who love God, to those who are the called according to His purpose." (Romans 8:28)

There are many other stories in the Bible of how God used the trials people faced to bring something good into their lives. It does not matter how much you have messed up or what you did since you were born again. If you make the choice to come back to God, He will make all things new.

Chapter 6

RELATIONSHIPS AND GOD'S TIMING

"Now therefore, I pray, if I have found grace in Your sight, show me now Your way, that I may know You and that I may find grace in Your sight..." Exodus 33:13

IT IS IMPERATIVE TO UNDERSTAND THE IMPORTANCE OF YOUR RE-LATIONSHIPS, BOTH WITH GOD AND OTHER PEOPLE, WHEN YOU MOVE FROM ONE SEASON OF YOUR LIFE TO ANOTHER. Each season brings an end to some relationships and the beginning of some new relationships. *Each season requires some new relationships.* Often new seasons start with or because of a new relationship. **This is the third sign by which God introduces new seasons and timing to us**. God accomplishes most purposes on this earth through relationship or divine connection. One of the most important things in the Kingdom of God is relationship. Most of the problems we face on this earth are relational. We are going to look at how each new season brings new levels of relationship with God and other people.

RELATIONSHIP WITH GOD

With each new season, we enter a new level of relationship with God. God desires an intimate and mature relationship with each of us. One of the purposes of God taking us from one season to another is to teach us how to trust Him and depend on Him more. There is a difference here between how things work in the natural and in the spirit.

In the natural, as children mature they do not depend on their parents as they did when they were younger. It is the desire of every parent for their children to grow up and move out of their house and form their own families. As children grow older, their relationship with their parents gets more distant and independent even though they love and respect them.

In the spirit, it is the other way around. The more we grow in God, the more we depend on Him and get closer to Him. The more we grow in Him, the more He wants to have an intimate relationship with us. In the spirit, the closer you are to God and the more you trust Him, the more mature you become. Each season in life is programmed that way by God. You will never become independent from your relationship with Him. He is your heavenly Father and the closer the relationship you desire with Him, the more you'll enjoy your life on this earth.

The disciples of Jesus had to learn, too. Jesus was with them for three and a half years physically. Towards the end of His ministry, Jesus told the disciples He had to go to the cross and go to His Father, leaving them on this earth. They did not expect to hear that from Him. They thought they were going to be with Him forever.

In a sense it was true, but they had to grow up and enter a new level of relationship with Him. They enjoyed traveling with Him and hearing Him teach and preach. They could touch and feel Him and He never left them unless He went away to pray. He took care of them for three and a half years and they did not have to work to make their living. Now He was leaving them. They could not digest that and could not believe that was going to happen.

When Jesus was arrested, they all ran away from Him, saddened and disappointed. While Jesus was with them, He said that it was for their advantage that He was going away (John 16:7). But they wanted to feel Him and touch Him physically and be with Him like they used to. They could still be with Jesus even though He was going away, but this had to occur on a new level. It was Jesus' desire to live *in* them, not only to be *with* them. When He was on this earth it was not possible for Him to live in them. In a way it is better for us to have Him living inside of us than having Him physically around us. We are created to be a temple of God and live in intimate communion with Him all the time.

I believe the biggest problem the disciples faced when Jesus left them was His physical absence. He promised that He would never leave them nor forsake them (John 14:18). They had to grow up in the spirit and learn how to relate with Him more deeply than they had when He was physically present with them. Though they were physically distant from Him, they entered a new relationship in the spirit that was closer than what they had enjoyed physically. That was the beginning of a new season in their lives.

In the Old Testament, when God brought the Israelites out of Egypt to take them to the Promised Land He led them through the wilderness. While they were in the wilderness, God appointed a cloud to be over them to guide them and a pillar of fire at night to show them the way. He fed them with manna while they were in the wilderness and they did not have to sow, plant, cook, or clean. It was safe and easy for them.

They became comfortable with it and were not that eager to go into the Promised Land. But God wanted them to go into the land and inherit their blessings. The Bible says the cloud and the pillar of fire were with them until they reached the Promised Land and the manna was stopped only after they crossed the Jordan.

> "For the cloud of the LORD was above the tabernacle by day,
> and fire was over it by night, in the sight of all the house of
> Israel, throughout all their journeys." (Exodus 40:38)

"Then the manna ceased on the day after they had eaten the produce of the land; and the children of Israel no longer had manna, but they ate the food of the land of Canaan that year." (Joshua 5:12)

When they reached the Promised Land, they entered a new season and God wanted to bring them to a new level of relationship with Him. Each new level requires a higher dimension of faith. He wants us to walk by faith and not by sight. He wants us to trust in Him and His Word and not depend on our feelings. In each new season, we enter into a new level of prayer and worship, and the Word becomes more alive and powerful to us.

One of the reasons we feel from time to time that God is distant from us is because He wants us to trust Him and believe in Him in spite of what we feel. If we are to mature, it is crucial that we know our relationship with God does not vary based on how we feel on a particular day.

RELATIONSHIP WITH PEOPLE

When God wants you to change in some areas, He will send a person (or a problem) to your life and they will be the catalyst of that change. There are areas in your life that need to change in order for God to use you. In the natural, you may have no knowledge or revelation about those areas. Sometimes the relationship with that person that God sends will cause those areas to manifest or surface in your life. When it comes to change, most people will be in denial for a while and resist until they receive a revelation from God.

Even love can be painful at times if two emotionally wounded people try to love each other. Sometimes the connection between your old and new season is a person or relationship. If you are married I am not advocating extra-marital relationships. That is not the kind of relationship I am talking about here. It is never God's will for you to have extra-marital relationships, physically or emotionally.

When God wants to promote you spiritually and financially He will either send an enemy to persecute you, or a friend to bless you. Most people do not like enemies and they try to avoid or run away from them.

Goliath was an enemy and he threatened the life of anyone who would challenge him. David saw Goliath not as an enemy but as an opportunity for promotion. What if David was afraid of Goliath and did not face him? He might have continued as a shepherd boy for the rest of his life. I am not saying God will send an enemy all the time. Sometimes it is just a person; for instance, Elijah was sent to the widow in Zarephath. Jesus was sent to the fishermen in Galilee.

The relationships you have in childhood will change as you reach adolescence. Though you may have the same people as friends, there could be a change in the level of friendship. And, of course, when you get married you enter into a new season of your life. This season begins because of the new level of relationship you started.

Relationships have a lot to do with spiritual timing. Whether or not you continue the old relationships, every new season will bring new ones. So, you must be open to receive the people whom God will send your way. God brings people because He works through people. Most of the problems and blessings you have on this earth will be with people and will come through people.

When God wants to change you, He brings people who will aggravate your heart and irritate the exact place where God wants you to change. You will think they are your enemies, but they are your teachers or mentors that reveal hidden areas of your heart and intentions that need to come in line with God's Word.

There are two kinds of people God will bring into your life in every new season. One will be to bless you and support you and give you uncommon favor. The other group will be to change you and prepare you for the next season, and it will be through friction and challenges. Paul had these two groups throughout his ministry. One group believed him and supported his ministry, and the other always opposed and attacked him.

You need both of these groups to fulfill your purpose. Neither is more important than the other one, though we do not like to be around those who reveal our weaknesses. Enemies will either reveal your weakness (to remind you that you are not perfect) or propel you to your divine destiny. Jesus needed Peter *and* Judas to fulfill His destiny. Without Judas Jesus would not have reached the cross. Do not hate the Judas in your life.

Each season begins with a new connection. Joseph was sold as a slave to Potiphar, but he was his new connection for his new season. Potiphar was a key person because he threw Joseph into the prison by the palace. There were other prisons in other parts of Egypt, but in order for Joseph to fulfill his purpose he had to be in the same prison as the baker and the cupbearer of the king.

When he was in prison, Joseph had to be with those two people out of all the other prisoners that were in there; maybe hundreds of them. That was the beginning of a new season for Joseph and that connection with those two prisoners helped him to get to the palace. Do you see how other people play a very significant role in helping you fulfill your purpose?

God send Elijah to meet Elisha to anoint him as his successor. I do not believe they knew each other before. Elisha's life was totally changed from the moment he met Elijah. His life entered a new season as a result (1 Kings 19:16). The disciples were fishermen until they met Jesus. When He called them to be His disciples they entered a new relationship with Jesus and they entered a new season in their lives. It is interesting to notice when we enter into a new relationship that God ordains both parties to enter into a new season in their lives simultaneously.

God will send different people for different purposes in different seasons of your life. Some will be to bless you spiritually, others financially, and still others with their wisdom and experience. In my own life, I have seen God send particular people to promote me in the Kingdom. My first financial breakthrough came because I was obedient to God and stepped out to support a missionary with ten rupees when I did not have ten rupees. If I had not met this brother in India and decided to help him, I would not be here today at this season in my life.

God used the ministry of a respected evangelist to touch my life in the beginning of my Christian walk. It was the beginning of a new season in my life. I got a tape of one of his messages from a friend of mine in India and I was attracted to his anointing. I never saw him or heard of him before, but just listening to him preach on an audiotape sparked something in me.

When he came to Mumbai, India, I traveled in a train for three days and took two of my friends to attend his conference. We had to sleep on the floor at night with over a hundred people in a hall. I got some of his books and more tapes and entered into a spiritual relationship with his ministry. You do not need to know someone personally to have a relationship in the spirit. Sometimes it will be strictly a spiritual relationship.

After I came to the US, I attended some more of his meetings and became a partner of his ministry. I never met him personally but his ministry blessed me in that season. Now I am in a new season of my life and I do not have the same relationship with him that I had in my last season.

One day I invited a man into our church in India to minister. After his first preaching we felt a connection in the spirit and we began to meet for prayer and fellowship quite often. He became my prayer and fasting partner. He was a convert from the Hindu religion and he had a passion for God that was deeper than anyone I knew at that time. It was the beginning of a new season in my life.

We fasted together for 3 days, 7 days, and twenty-one days several times. We would travel together by train and go to a city and fast and pray. It was a wonderful time of growth and maturing in the things of God. During one of those times of fasting, I wrote my first two books and part of my third book. I could count on him for prayer.

Then we started our new church in our town and during one of those times of fasting God said my time with this friend would be coming to an end. Before that word, many people were jealous of our relationship and tried to break our friendship but I did not feel in my spirit that it was the right time. But this time I felt it in my spirit and it was one of the hardest moments in both of our lives.

I had to put some distance between us and even though I see him often, we do not have the same kind of relationship we used to have. That was a different season and I do not need that kind of friendship now. You need to know when to let go of relationships when you enter into a new season. That does not mean you need to be completely cut off from that person unless it was an illegal, illicit, or unhealthy relationship.

David had different people as his friends in different seasons of his life. When he was in the palace before he became king, Jonathan played a key role in his life. But, it was for a season. After he became king he had other prophets, captains, mighty men and priests in the palace as his friends.

The Apostle Paul also had different relationships in different seasons of his life. After Paul's conversion God sent Ananias to help start his Christian walk. Then, God sent him Barnabas to introduce him to the original apostles who were in Jerusalem. I believe the friendship with Barnabas was only for a season, although it did not need to end the way it did. Afterward, Silas became his partner on his missionary journeys. Some of us still try to keep our Ananias or Barnabas with us and they are hindering us from entering into new seasons in the spirit.

When Abraham obeyed God's call and started out on his journey he took his nephew Lot with him. They could only continue their journey for a while and then they had to separate. If he had not separated from Lot, Abraham would not have met Melchizedek. Very seldom will God keep people in your life that you know from your birth. You will have family and acquaintances that last for a lifetime, but most of the active relationships are seasonal.

I have learned one very important lesson in my life: If your problem was caused by people, then God will use other people to solve that problem. If your problem was caused by supernatural or evil forces, then God will solve that problem.

Until I was twenty-six years old I had no idea about Christian counseling. I never knew that such a ministry existed. I believed that every miracle or healing you need must come supernaturally from God, and if He hadn't performed it you had to keep believing and do more fasting. I realized that one of the names of Jesus is Wonderful Counselor (Isaiah 9:6). One of the Spirits of the Lord is called the Spirit of Counsel (Isaiah 11:2). In fact, some healing that people need can come only by receiving godly counseling, especially if it has to do with your soul or past behavior.

Most people go to God to help them with problems other people have caused. It is good to ask Him, but He will send a man or a woman your way to help you find the solution. You can pray and pray for years and you may be expecting God to do something supernatural. I can tell you it may not happen. For example, if you were abused by someone when you were a child, your healing will probably come through a counselor who is equipped to deal with such things.

I believe everyone in the body of Christ needs to go through some kind of counseling or healing process for their souls. Because we all grew up in some kind of dysfunctional family, our spiritual and mental development was affected. It is causing us dysfunction in one way or another.

The reason we are not able to experience what the Bible says we should experience is because our souls are not prospering in those areas. The prosperity we experience depends on the prosperity we have in our souls (3 John 2). Throughout the Bible, God talks about different types of counseling; whose counsel you should follow and whose you should not (Psalm 1:1). Since realizing that God uses human counselors to meet some needs, I have been blessed with different people whom God used to give me godly counsel, especially in my marriage and ministry life.

In different seasons of your life God will use different ministries to bless you and teach you what you need to learn. Each minister has a different revelation and manifestation of the grace of God. Sometimes it will be a spiritual relationship you have with a particular ministry. You cannot receive all you need from one preacher.

What if one part of your body kept growing and the others did not? What if we keep eating only one kind of food all the time? Our body will not get the nutrients it needs and it will be deformed. We need a balanced diet. Your spirit needs exposure to different types of anointing to mature in the Lord. That is why God has put five-fold ministries in the Church; Apostles, Prophets, Evangelists, Pastors and Teachers (Ephesians 4:11). Every minister within the five ministry offices carries a different anointing, though they all are ministers of the gospel. At some point in life you need to sit under each of them and learn from them in order to grow to be a mature person in Christ.

There is nothing more important in the Kingdom than relationships. If you want to know more about the power and importance of relationships and how they affect your prosperity, please read my book, *Overcoming the*

Spirit of Poverty.

Sometimes people miss their relationship because it does not come in the package (outward appearance) they expected. What does that mean? God sent the solution to humanity's problem with the birth and ministry of Jesus. The people of His time did not recognize or receive Him because He did not come in a way they expected a deliverer or a king to come. He did not look the way they expected Him to look and did not do what they wanted someone like Him to do.

Let me tell you, sometimes God hides His most precious treasures in dirt that no one will even notice unless they take a deeper look at it. In the natural, most precious metals and stones are hidden in the dirt. Paul said, "But we have this treasure in earthen vessels, that the excellence of the power may be of God and not of us." (2 Corinthians 4:7)

God has put more honor on those members of the body whom we think are not honorable so that we will care for one another. 1 Corinthians 12:23-26 says,

> "And those members of the body which we think to be less honorable, on these we bestow greater honor; and our unpresentable parts have greater modesty, but our presentable parts have no need. But God composed the body, having given greater honor to that part which lacks it, that there should be no schism in the body, but that the members should have the same care for one another. And if one member suffers, all the members suffer with it; or if one member is honored, all the members rejoice with it."

Just as God sends other people to bless you and promote you, He will send you to bless and promote others. I know a few people God sent me to help, but they did not receive me because I did not come in the package they expected their help to come. Naaman was sent to Elisha to receive his healing of leprosy. Naaman almost missed it, and would have if it hadn't been for his servants, because Elisha did not do what Naaman expected him to do (2 Kings 5:1-14).

God may send people from different cultures, colors, and languages to help you and be the catalyst to fulfill your purpose. You need to be open to accept and receive from them as if you are receiving directly from God.

DANGER OF WRONG RELATIONSHIPS

Relationships can bring blessings or destruction into our lives. As the Bible says, dead flies can stink up the ointment (Ecclesiastes 10:1). We need to be careful with whom we associate. The same way God sends relationships to promote us, the enemy sends wrong relationships to distract us. The enemy can send people into our paths to hinder us from entering into our new season and fulfilling God's purpose for our lives. If you enter into relationships with people that are not God's will, you will delay your progress and bring unnecessary problems into your life. What differentiates these two relationships is the peace in your heart. When God sends someone to you or sends you to someone you will have the peace of God in your heart and spirit.

You may not find too many people whom you can trust. If you can find one person in your life that you can trust and will be faithful to you, it will be a great blessing. In Paul's ministry, he found only one person who was like-minded and faithful and that was Timothy (Philippians 2:19-20).

There are many examples in the Bible where people perished because of their wrong associations. God rejected many kings in the Old Testament because they entered into relationship with other kings and people with whom God did not want them to relate; Solomon (1 Kings 11:1-8); Rehoboam (1 Kings 12:8-16); Asa (2 Chronicles 16:7-9); Jehoshaphat (2 Chronicles 18:1; 19:2; 20:35-37); Ahab (1 Kings 21:25). Joshua entered into a covenant with the Gibeonites without asking God's counsel (Joshua 9:3-16). Make sure you hear from God before you enter into a deeper level of relationship with someone in life, either in business or ministry, or personally.

Chapter 7

Revelation and God's Timing

"The unfolding of your words gives light; it gives understanding to the simple." Psalm 119:130 (NIV)

EACH NEW SEASON IN LIFE COMES WITH A NEW REVELATION OF GOD. What I mean by revelation is that you will know something about God that you did not know before. This will usher you into your new season. **This is the fourth sign God uses to communicate His timing.** I do not believe that anyone who has lived or is still living on this earth has known everything there is to know of God.

The Bible says, "The fear of the Lord is the beginning of wisdom and knowledge of the Holy One is understanding" (Proverbs 9:10). One of the main reasons we go from one season to another is to get to know God.

We see in the Old Testament a progression of God's revelation from one generation to the next generation. Abraham knew God a little more than Noah knew Him. Moses knew God more than Abraham knew Him, etc.

I am not talking about receiving extra-Biblical revelation. Revelation is the unveiling of truth that is already in the Bible, but you never knew or applied to your life before. Sometimes what you need to fulfill your destiny is a relationship or a revelation. One of the ways the enemy works in the lives of many believers is by making them spiritually complacent or giving them a false sense of, "I know it all." One of the best ways to receive new revelation of the Word is to pray Paul's prayer for the Ephesian church (Ephesians 1:17-23).

The revelation that you receive in each new season will be your strength and weapon against the enemy. You might have heard the phrase, 'new level, new devil.' What is meant by that is that when you go to a new level in life you will have to face new enemies. I want to say here, 'new level, new revelation.' To face the enemy in your new season God will equip you with new revelation knowledge. You will defeat all of your spiritual foes with that one revelation. When God appeared to Moses on Mount Horeb, He revealed Himself as He had never revealed Himself to anyone before. He said I AM that I AM sending you to Egypt. God never told that to anyone before. In Exodus 6:2-3 we read,

> "And God spake unto Moses, and said unto him, I am the LORD: And I appeared unto Abraham, unto Isaac, and unto Jacob, by the name of God Almighty, but by my name JEHOVAH was I not known to them." (KJV)

Here we see God revealing something about Himself that He never revealed to anyone before. It was not just a name that He was revealing here, but what that name consists of. Everything that God is, God has, and God does is contained in His name. We know God by His name. We receive from God through His name. We have relationship with God through His name. We call Him by His name. God does everything by His name, through His name, and for His name.

God equipped Moses spiritually to face Pharaoh and the spiritual forces that were ruling Egypt. Moses never thought he could deliver Israel from slavery. He wanted to bail out of God's call. One of the reasons Moses denied the call was because he was thinking about it naturally. He knew about his weaknesses and the military power Pharaoh had. For him to go to Egypt to deliver his people, he would have to defeat Pharaoh and his army and he knew there was no way that was possible. Later, he found out the revelation he had of God at the mountain was more powerful than the enemy he had to face. With that revelation he entered a new season in his life.

All biblical miracles are tied to the revelation of God's name. Jesus said He came to reveal the Father to us (John 14:9). How did He reveal the Father to us? He did that through His works. He said He did the works that He saw His Father doing. Whatever He did was a manifestation of one of God's names. Whether it was healing the sick, delivering the demon-possessed, or feeding the hungry; all were manifestations of one of God's names.

In John 17:6 & 26 we read,

> "I have manifested Your name to the men whom You have giv-en Me out of the world. . . and I have declared to them Your name, and will declare it."

Jesus is saying that during His earthly ministry He revealed the Father's name to the people whom the Father gave Him.

Though I grew up in a Christian home, I never knew I could trust God for financial miracles and actually sow a seed in faith and expect a harvest. It is a truth mentioned in the Bible but it did not benefit me because I did not have a revelation about it. Those kinds of things were not taught in my church. When the time came to receive the offering the pastor never said a word from the Bible about offering or finances. However, Jesus taught exhaustively about money and financial matters.

In India, the people have a poverty mentality. When they think about giving to God they usually give the least and not the best. Most of the nominal churches and Hindu temples and mosques have an altar built outside the building, mostly on the roadside, where people can put their offerings.

People are most likely to give when they go someplace to buy something new—they treat their offering like a good luck charm. They will throw some coins, even from the passing trucks, buses, or cars as they drive by. Sometimes it hits other people and there have actually been some who lost their eyes because the flying coins hit them in the eyes. Anyway, to make a long story short, they think God is in need of some coins from their pocket because He needs some money to buy food. It is a mockery to God, and it is keeping them poor because the Bible says that whatever a man sows he shall reap.

When I entered the ministry, I did not have a revelation about prosperity or financial breakthroughs. I believed that if I did not have any money, then I did not have any money and I could not do anything about it. But that changed in 1995 when I was with a team in North India preaching the gospel.

My team leader was a Hindu convert. There was no one supporting this brother and he did not have any income even to buy toiletries. At the end of our ministry, he asked if I would support him ten rupees per month, which is about twenty cents in American dollars. I did not have ten rupees in my hand and I did not know what to say. Suddenly, the Holy Spirit gave me faith in my heart and I said to him, "Brother, if God gives me ten rupees by next month, I will send it to you."

I went back home and he went to his place. The next month, God gave me ten rupees because He gave me an idea to do some work for someone. I sent that money to my friend and the next month God gave me thirty rupees. I said, "Wow, this is working!" and I sent him those thirty rupees. The next month He gave me sixty and it kept increasing every month until it reached 1,500 rupees a month. God said that I would never run out of money in my wallet and it has been true to this day.

This experience opened my eyes to something I had never known. Even though the principle of sowing and reaping has always been in the Bible, no one had ever taught it to me before. I had heard the story of the widow and Elijah; how she gave him what she had and was blessed, but I did not know if that could happen to me. That revelation was the beginning of a new season in my financial life.

Another example I want to share with you is about a time I was invited to preach at a church in the US. When I reached there, I had only three dollars cash in my wallet. When the offering time came, the Holy Spirit told me to give it all. I obeyed and gave the three dollars I had. After the service, one lady came to shake my hands and she put fifty dollars in my hand. That is called a Pentecostal Handshake!

The next day, one family invited me to have lunch with them and on the way back from lunch this man stopped at the bank and took two hundred dollars cash and blessed me. When I was leaving, the pastor of the church said they had a check for me and it was the largest single offering I had ever received from a church.

Do not misunderstand me. This is not a spiritual gimmick. God wants you to be blessed in every way. But, if you will not believe that God can bless you in an area of your life, He will not bless you in that area. What works for you in the Bible is what you *believe* in the Bible. Also, you need to release something in faith because without faith it is impossible to please Him.

Paul says in the epistles that whatever a man sows he shall reap. Those who sow sparingly will reap sparingly and those who sow bountifully shall reap bountifully (2 Corinthians 9:6). Also, he said that whatever does not originate in faith is sin (Romans 14:23b).

We read in the Bible about Jacob and how he had to run away from his house (Genesis 27:43) for fear of Esau. He was alone and had nothing as a personal possession. He left Beersheba and went toward Haran and the Bible says he tarried at a certain place that night and had a dream (Genesis 28:10-15). Through that dream he had a revelation of the God of his fathers; Isaac and Abraham.

That revelation led Jacob to make a faith commitment to give God a tithe (a tenth) of everything with which God blessed him. At the time He did not have anything to give to God, but He had faith in his heart based on what he heard from Him. There is nothing more powerful than giving something to God by faith when you do not have it.

In truth, Jacob paid a tithe by faith before he had any income. That honored God, and after a few years God blessed him and he became a wealthy man. Genesis 30:43 says, "Thus the man [Jacob] became exceedingly prosperous, and had large flocks, female and male servants, and camels and donkeys."

In Genesis 32:10, Jacob said, "...for I crossed over this Jordan with my staff, and now I have become two companies." That is the power of giving by faith, which is the secret to financial prosperity. I will say more about this in the next chapter with regard to "Sowing and God's timing."

Our God is a God of abundance and there is no lack in Him. But, how much we receive from Him depends on our faith. If we do not put our faith to work we cannot receive any benefit. Faith without works is dead. Some people confuse faith with believing or feeling. Please read Hebrews 11:1 & James 2:17-20 again.

All provision for the ministry we do comes by trusting in God's faithfulness and sowing seeds by faith into various other ministries and lives. There will be divine moments when God will tell you to give something to someone and, if you obey, there will be a blessing.

I have found that we will not receive a financial miracle without sacrificial giving. In the Old and New Testaments we see that whenever and wherever people gave sacrificially, they received a miracle. The widow during Elijah's time gave the last meal she had and was supernaturally blessed.

The boy with the five loaves and two fishes gave it all to Jesus and received a miracle that fed five thousand people. I believe the 12 baskets that were left were sent to that boy's home. Jesus noticed the widow who gave her last two mites and commented about her giving (Luke 21:1-4).

When you go through a tough season, be open to receive and know God in a way that you never knew Him before. Every new season comes with a new challenge and every new challenge comes with a new revelation of God. We saw in Moses' life how he entered his new season with a new revelation. We see that also with Abraham in Genesis. After he went to rescue his nephew Lot from the enemies, Abraham had an encounter with God. On the way back from the battle, Melchizedek, the King of Salem and the priest of the Lord, came and greeted him.

I believe it was Jesus who appeared to Abraham and they had communion together. Melchizedek brought bread and wine and blessed Abraham. I believe Abraham had this encounter because he risked his own life to rescue Lot. He could have sent some hired servants to go and fight against the enemies. He went himself and took his own servants. Afterward, Abraham gave a tithe to Melchizedek and it was a new beginning for him (Genesis 14:18-20).

If the disciples of Jesus had not gone through their season of great pain and disappointment when He left the earth, they would not have seen the day of Pentecost. Forty days after the ascension of Jesus they entered into a new season in their lives. With the coming of the Holy Spirit the disciples received a new revelation of God they never had before; that no one ever had before. To this day we are enjoying that revelation they received on the day of Pentecost.

Though Jesus commanded the disciples to be witnesses for Him in Jerusalem, Judea, Samaria and the uttermost parts of the earth, they were not willing to go outside of Jerusalem, nor were they willing to share the gospel with any Gentiles. Peter had a revelation from God through a trance to reach out to the Gentiles (Acts 10:10-16). That was the beginning of a new season for the whole church.

We all love the book of Revelation and we know that the Apostle John received that revelation. Sometimes we forget the background and where he was when he received that powerful revelation from Jesus Christ. He was exiled by the Roman emperor to the isle of Patmos. It was not a place you would go for a vacation. It was a desert and only wild animals lived on that island. They sent people there to die and never expected them to live or come back again.

It has been said that one of the reasons they sent John to Patmos was because they tried to kill him by putting him in boiling oil, but he did not die. At last, they decided to send him to this island. Humanly speaking, it was a painful experience and sheer torture to be there. But, on the Lord's Day, John was in the spirit and Jesus revealed to him everything that was going to take place from then on.

The future of this world was revealed to him. He received that revelation in the midst of his great pain and suffering. He may have had no food or water for days and no one with whom to fellowship. No cell phone to call home. No electricity or sanitation of any kind. Maybe there was not even a roof over his head. God had to take him to that island to give him that revelation. Let me share with you; the greater the purpose, the greater the pain you go through; and the greater the pain, the greater the revelation.

We have seen that Paul received a new revelation of God when he was struck down to the ground by Jesus. Prior to that his faith was based on the revelation he had of the Old Testament. He had to go through that pain of blindness and humbling to receive a revelation of who Jesus is.

I believe Paul knew this secret in his life, the secret that many new seasons come with pain and that pain brings new revelation. That is why he instructed us to rejoice always. We see him rejoicing and praising God and writing great epistles to the churches from the prison. Some of his masterpiece epistles, like Ephesians and Philippians, were written while he was in prison. He received those powerful revelations about Christ and the Church in the midst of his pain and great suffering.

Chapter 8

SOWING AND GOD'S TIMING

"Those who sow in tears shall reap in joy." Psalm 126:5

REMEMBER, DIFFERENT SEASONS START WITH THE REVELATION OF DIFFERENT SPIRITUAL PRINCIPLES. Here I want to mention one of the main keys that God uses to promote people in His Kingdom. It is through sowing financial or material seeds. **This is the fifth sign He uses to communicate His timing to us.** One of the greatest desires God has for your life is that He wants to bless other people through you.

I believe with all my heart that we will not enter into some of the greatest seasons in our life until we obey God in some critical moments of financial and material giving. What I mean by material giving is that He may ask you to give away cars, houses, or anything that is of monetary value. In the following pages, I will explain more about how sowing financial seeds and blessing others will open the doors of a new season in your life, which otherwise would not open.

Until you loose something on this earth by faith, nothing will be loosed in heaven (Matthew 18:18). Especially when going from one financial season to another; from one financial level to another, the key is to sow a sacrificial seed when God prompts your spirit. We see this principle at work throughout the Bible. It is not the invention of prosperity preachers; it is a pivotal truth of God's Word. Much of what Jesus preached dealt with money-related or financial investment subjects. He preached about this more than He preached about prayer, faith, heaven or hell.

Genesis 8:22 reads,

> "While the earth remains, seedtime and harvest, cold and heat, winter and summer, and day and night shall not cease."

We read from the above scripture that sowing and reaping is a principle set by God on this earth. In the natural, there is a season for sowing and a season for reaping (harvesting). I grew up near a rice field and every year I used to watch the process of sowing and harvesting rice.

Before the farmer sows the rice he has to prepare the ground. It is very hard work that is not accomplished in one day. He has to stand under the scourging heat of the sun the whole time and when he is done for the day he is exhausted and ready to go to bed. He has to sow the rice seeds before the Monsoon starts, otherwise he will not have anything to harvest when the harvest time comes.

Another important truth we learn from the above scriptures is that there is a 'time' for sowing the seed and a 'time' between the sowing and the harvest. You do not sow your seeds anytime you want and anywhere you want. There is a particular time, place and weather required for different seeds. There is a season for sowing and a season of harvesting. The same principle applies in the spirit. The sowing time is a time of pain, just as it says in the Psalm, "Those who sow in tears shall reap in joy" (Psalm 126:5). I believe what determines the length of time between sowing and the harvest season is the size of the seed sown. The smaller the seed, the faster you receive the harvest, and the bigger the seed, the longer it takes for a harvest.

The state where I grew up in India is called Kerala, which means the "land of coconuts." I remember my father used to plant coconut seeds in our back yard and wait for the seeds to germinate. Coconut is a large seed in size and it takes three months to germinate. It takes five to seven years for the coconut tree to grow and produce the harvest.

In the natural there is a particular time for sowing and if someone misses that season, they will not receive any harvest. It is also true in the spirit. There are particular times and seasons in life that God inspires us to sow into other people's lives and ministries. And, if we obey, we will receive a harvest.

Ecclesiastes 3:2 says,

"A time to plant and a time to harvest." (NLT)

Whatever you have today financially, spiritually, or in relationship, is the harvest of the seed you planted in your last season. The Bible says in Galatians 6:7, "Do not be deceived, God is not mocked; for whatever a man sows, that he will also reap."

YOUR GIVING IS IMPORTANT TO GOD

Your giving determines how God responds to your need. Your giving determines how God will cause other people to show you favor. Favor is God causing other people to bless you unexpectedly when you are not qualified for the blessing. God's favor will take you places where nothing else can.

The first murder on this earth took place as someone reacted to the favor giving had brought to someone else's life. We read in Genesis 4:3-8 that Cain brought the offering first to God and He did not respect Cain's offering. Then Abel brought an offering, the firstborn of his flock and of their fat. God respected Abel's offering, which brought jealousy in Cain's heart. When they were in the field, Cain killed his brother Abel. Your giving, and the favor that comes as a result, creates a reaction in the spirit world. God takes your giving seriously.

After the Israelites reached the Promised Land the first judgment against them concerned giving. God gave Joshua specific orders that when they invaded Jericho, the first fortified city in the Promised Land, every bit of wealth; gold, silver, vessels of bronze and iron, was to be consecrated to the LORD and they were to bring it all to the treasury of the LORD (Joshua 6:19). No man was allowed to touch it or take anything from it. But Achan disobeyed, taking some of the money and hiding it in the camp, and sinned against the LORD.

God said in Joshua 7:11,

> "Israel has sinned, and they have also transgressed My covenant which I commanded them. For they have even taken some of the accursed things, and have both stolen and deceived; and they have also put it among their own stuff."

It was a serious crime against the LORD. Israel could not stand against their enemies and was defeated by the people of Ai. They restituted the crime by stoning Achan and his family and God restored His favor upon Israel. Your giving determines your victory over your enemies. Your giving can determine how God will allow your enemies to treat you.

The first judgment in the New Testament church was about giving. A family in the early church sold their possession and kept back part of the money. They brought the rest to the apostles in Acts chapter 5:1-11. When they brought the money, they lied to Peter, saying what they gave was all of the money received from selling their property. The Bible says Ananias fell down dead and people took him and buried him. Three hours later his wife, Sapphira, came and Peter asked her about the money and she lied to him. She fell down dead and the people buried her next to her husband.

It amazes me how seriously God considers our heart when we give to Him. It is a matter of life and death; curse and blessing. When I first read Acts chapter 5 about Ananias and Sapphira, I was shocked that God would judge someone in the New Testament about giving. I had to ask God to forgive me for not respecting Him with my giving.

The door for the ministry to the Gentiles was opened because of the giving of a man called Cornelius. Acts 10:1-2 says,

> "There was a certain man in Caesarea called Cornelius, a cen-

turion of what was called the Italian Regiment, a devout man and one who feared God with all his household, who gave alms generously to the people, and prayed to God always."

God noted Cornelius' prayers and giving. That caused Him to send Peter to his house to preach the gospel to him and his household. He was the first fruit of the Gentile believers and the Bible says he was a generous man. Your giving can determine your salvation and the salvation of your household. Thank God for Cornelius and his giving; if it hadn't been for him, we might not have received the gospel.

Cornelius had a vision of an angel and we need to notice what the angel told him. Acts 10:4 says,

> "And when he observed him, he was afraid, and said, "What is it, lord?" So he said to him, "Your prayers and your alms have come up for a memorial before God."

This scripture tells us again that God notices not just our prayers but our giving, and He keeps a record of what we give to Him and His Kingdom.

To receive a breakthrough, it does not always have to be money that you give. Anything that costs you; your time, material possessions, opportunity, food, water, etc. can be the tool. When you give sacrificially to someone in need, it can unlock a new season in the spirit.

From the beginning, we see that when a person gives wholeheartedly to someone else or to God, it invokes God's favor to manifest in their lives. It is not because God is in need of something from us, but He is a God of love and love always gives until it hurts. When a man or woman's life shows that nature of God to others, it pleases Him to move on their behalf.

We see in Genesis chapter 4 about the sacrifices Cain and Abel brought to God. God was pleased with Abel's offering and rejected Cain's. One of the reasons was because Abel brought the best of what he had to God. It cost him something to give that offering. If an offering does not cost you anything and does not get registered in your heart when you give it, it will not be registered in heaven.

When you look back, the offerings and gifts that you remember are those

God remembers because they were valuable to you. If you want something valuable from God, you need to release something valuable from your hand or from your life on this earth.

In Luke 21, we read about a widow who put two mites into the offering. Jesus noticed and commented on her offering. There were many rich people who gave big offerings, maybe thousands of dollars, but none of them were noticed by Jesus.

> "And He looked up and saw the rich putting their gifts into the treasury, and He saw also a certain poor widow putting in two mites. So He said, "Truly I say to you that this poor widow has put in more than all; for all these out of their abundance have put in offerings for God, but she out of her poverty put in all the livelihood that she had." (Luke 21:1-4)

When Noah came out of the ark after the flood, the first thing he did was offer a sacrifice to God. He built an altar to the Lord and took some of every clean animal and clean fowl and offered burnt offerings on the altar (Genesis 8:20-21). I believe it cost Noah to make that offering and he took time to build an altar. He did not try to build himself a house, but he put God first in his life and God came down and blessed Noah and the earth (Genesis 9:1).

We have studied Abraham's life in detail, but I want to mention one more time how critical it was for him to invite the *three strangers* he saw outside into his house and give them a great dinner, for the fulfillment of the promise God gave him concerning a son. He might have had other plans for the afternoon. He went out of his way and gave the Lord the best he had. Chapter 19 of Genesis starts with saying, "Then the LORD appeared to him by the terebinth trees..."

Abraham saw that three men were standing by him. He did not know that it was the LORD but he invited them into his house and offered to serve them. He prepared a delicious meal and brought it to them. Genesis 18:6-8 says, "So Abraham hurried into the tent to Sarah and said, "Quickly, make ready three measures of *fine meal*; knead it and make cakes."

And Abraham ran to the herd, took a tender and *good calf,* gave it to a young man, and he hastened to prepare it. So he took butter and milk and the calf which he had prepared, and set it before them; and he stood by them under the tree as they ate." (Italics added)

Abraham gave them the best without knowing he was giving to God Almighty, and after the meal they blessed him and Sarah and said, "I will certainly return to you according to the time of life, and behold, Sarah your wife shall have a son" (Genesis 18:10). They entered a new season as a result of their giving.

Genesis 18:14 says,

> "Is anything too hard for the Lord? At the *appointed time* I will return to you, according to the *time of life,* and Sarah shall have a son." (Italics added)

As the LORD said, in the following year they had Isaac. Abraham's destiny would not have been completed unless he was obedient and willing to give Isaac. He had only one son and he waited for him almost his entire life. He was willing to give that up and inherited the blessing. I do not believe Abraham would ever forget the experience of waiting. It was painful, but as the Bible says, obedience is better than sacrifice (1 Samuel 15:22).

Every pain you endure for God's sake or for His Kingdom will be multiplied back to you as a blessing. As the Bible says, "Give, and it will be given to you: good measure, pressed down, shaken together, and running over will be put into your bosom..." (Luke 6:38)

Before Abraham's death, he commanded his servant to go to his kindred to find a wife for his son Isaac. His servant took ten camels loaded with wealth and departed to Mesopotamia (Genesis 24:10). Abraham was a wealthy man with silver, gold, and all material blessings. The servant loaded the camels with gold and silver, gifts, and expensive clothing that might have been worth hundreds of thousands of dollars.

On the way, he prayed to God and asked for a sign (Genesis 24:12). He stopped by a well to get some water for himself and the camels. The sign he asked from God was that the girl who would give water to him and the camels also would be the girl that God had chosen for Isaac.

You may think it was the easiest thing to give water, but in those days it was not that easy. Drawing water from a well was hard work. I believe she might have come to get water for her animals or for her household, which was enough work in itself. Again, drawing for someone else and for his animals was not an easy task.

I know this because when I was growing up we did not have an electric motor or running water in my house. Each house had a well and it was fifty to sixty feet deep. There was a pulley that was attached on top of the well and you used a long rope tied to a bucket to draw water. I used to do that for my mother every day, helping her to get water for use in the kitchen. It was good exercise and my arms grew stronger because of that.

As soon as he finished praying, Rebekah came and did exactly what he had asked. She gave more than what he asked for. He only asked her to give him water, but after she gave it to him, she also offered to draw water for his camels. That one act of giving changed her entire life. She was married to Isaac and inherited the entire wealth of Abraham.

What if she said, "I don't know this guy and I am not going to spend my time taking care of some stranger and his animals; I have my own work to do?" She would have missed her season and would not have inherited the blessing.

Do you see the pattern? When you do more than you are required to do, you will be blessed more than you deserve to be blessed. When you give more than what is required, you will inherit the abundance of God without any limit. As the Bible says, "For with the same measure that you use, it will be measured back to you." (Luke 6:38b)

There are many other examples in the Old Testament of how giving brought breakthroughs and deliverance to people. All of these people gave out of their need by faith or when God told them to give. Before the Israelites came out of Egypt, God asked them to observe the Passover. Every family was supposed to take a lamb that was without any blemish, apply its blood to the doorpost of their houses, and eat the meat as a family. The firstborn of everyone who did not observe the Passover perished. I believe that was an act of giving that protected them and destroyed the yoke of bondage over their lives.

We read in the book of Samuel about Hannah, who did not have a child and was despised by her family. She went into the house of God and prayed and made a commitment to God that if He would bless her with a male child, she would give that child back to Him (1 Samuel 1:11).

She believed God for a son and, before she even had him, she gave him to the Lord. The rest is history. God heard her prayer and Samuel was born a year later. After he was weaned, she took Samuel, three bullocks, one ephah of flour and a bottle of wine and brought them to the house of the Lord (1 Samuel 1:24).

Samuel grew up to be a mighty prophet of the Lord and brought Israel back from spiritual apostasy. God used Samuel to anoint Saul and David and institute kingship in Israel. Two books in the Bible are named after Samuel. This all happened because Hannah was willing to give up something that was precious to her. God honored that and blessed many other people through her.

Everyone knows about the wealth, glory, and wisdom of Solomon, but few know how he got it all. Solomon was not the wisest and wealthiest man when he became king. It all began when he went to Gibeon to sacrifice to the Lord. He offered an unusual sacrifice that day by giving one thousand burnt offerings (1 Kings 3:4-5).

That same night, the Lord appeared to him in a dream and asked him to make a request of God. Whatever he would have asked, the Lord would have given to Solomon. He asked for wisdom and understanding and God was pleased with his request (1 Kings 3:9-10).

This was the beginning of the greatness of Solomon. It all started with giving an unusual offering to the Lord. If you want unusual blessings, you need to give unusual offerings. If your offering does not cost you anything, do not expect to receive anything that is costly.

We know the story of the widow who gave a piece of bread to God's prophet Elijah. She was planning to die after eating the last piece of bread she and her son had (1 Kings 17:12). According to the Word of the Lord through the Prophet, she gave the last meal she and her son had to Elijah. I believe the reason she gave that to him was because previously God commanded this widow about the coming of the Prophet Elijah. When she heard the Word of the Lord through Elijah faith came into her heart, and she prepared it and brought it to him (1 Kings 17:14-16).

1 Kings 17:9 says,

> "Arise, go to Zarephath, which belongs to Sidon, and dwell there. See, I have commanded a widow there to provide for you."

As a result, she entered into a new season in her financial and material life which she never had before. She received an unusual blessing. Imagine how much it cost to give that piece of bread. It was her life and she had nothing left to eat.

One thing I have found in my life is that not everyone who gives receives an unusual blessing. The churches in the west are big about teaching on tithes. Many people give their tithe faithfully. I have found that not everyone who tithes receives unusual financial blessings.

I have known families who have tithed faithfully for many years and I have seen them struggle and face great financial difficulties. I used to wonder, "Lord, what is wrong? Your Word says that if we bring the tithe to the storehouse, you would open the windows of heaven and pour out a blessing that we are not able to contain."

If you study carefully the incidents where people received unusual financial breakthroughs, in the Bible and in the Church today, you will see people who obeyed the voice of the Lord and gave sacrificially in the midst of their great pain or lack. In the Old Testament they were commanded to bring tithes of money and produce of the ground. In the New Testament there is no such commandment, however we are commanded to give not just the usual tithes but to go the extra mile.

I am not saying here you should not pay your tithes. We pay tithes from our personal income and the ministry and give offerings above that. We know the New Testament emphasizes giving more than the Old Testament does. I believe the only offering that will bring a financial breakthrough is the offering that you give sacrificially according to God's timing and direction.

Most often, those times come in the midst of great financial struggle and lack. It is not easy to obey God at that time. God will present each of us with those moments in our lives and we need to be obedient to His Spirit. If you have missed a chance He will bring another opportunity.

In the New Testament we read about the boy who gave five loaves and two fishes to Jesus. Jesus blessed it and fed five thousand hungry men, besides women and children. When we release something to God, he multiplies that and will give it back to us; not just to bless us but to be a blessing to others. I have seen in my own life and ministry that every financial breakthrough was preceded by sacrificial giving.

There is a way to go from one level to the next financially. It is to give sacrificially. If you want to step into the next level of your financial blessing, watch out for what God is saying to you and obey it. Each level requires a higher level of sacrifice.

I started with sowing twenty cents by faith to support a missionary when I did not have it. Now I am beyond the thousand dollar limit in my one-time giving. It hurt when I gave my first thousand dollar offering. As I continued to use that faith muscle it got stronger and stronger and now it is not a pain at all. I would encourage you to do the same. God is waiting for you to step out and believe for the unusual.

I have given away cars, motor bikes, furniture, clothing, and helped build houses according to God's guidance, and God blessed me each time when I needed those in my own life. It was not easy to obey God when He asked me to give away some of those things. I had to go through great mental struggles to give away something that was very precious to me. You cannot expect to reap from an area in which you have not sown. When you sow, make sure you sow the best you have and not the used and broken.

In the natural, if you sow good seeds your harvest will be good. If you sow seeds that are unhealthy, they will not grow well or produce a good harvest. The better the seeds, the better the harvest. The quality of the seed determines the quality of the harvest.

I want to tell you from my experience that whenever I needed houses, cars, clothing, etc., God brought them to me. So far, whenever I move to a new city I have never had to look into the Apartment Finder for a place to live. The reason is because I have sown into that area in many people's lives and God is faithful to bring the harvest each time I have a need.

In the natural, if you sow papaya seeds you will reap papayas and not mangoes. Many people think differently in the spirit. They sow mango seeds and expect apples. What I mean by that is, they sow money *unintentionally* and *unexpectantly* and wait for what they need in their life to show up at their door.

Just because you sowed money does not mean you will reap a car. If you want a car, give away your old car or sow a seed to someone who needs a car. If you need a house, sow into someone who needs a house or help someone build a house. Again, I want to say that you cannot expect to reap where you have not sown. Remember the principle; *every seed reproduces its own kind.*

A seed is something that has unlimited potential to produce its own kind. As someone said, "You can count the seeds in an apple, but you cannot count the apples in a seed." Money is a seed and it is the only seed you can sow and expect to receive anything you want in your life.

In the spirit, you can sow money *intentionally* and *expectantly* toward something you are believing God to do for you. It can be sown toward material things like houses, cars, jobs, money, or for spiritual blessings. Money is a common seed that has the ability to reproduce what you assign and believe God for when you sow it in faith.

One of the most famous Bible verses is John 3:16. God had only one begotten Son and when the fullness of time came, He gave that Son to die on the cross. It is noted that it says *when* God gave His Son. He waited for the right time, meaning when the right time came in the spirit. That is why the Bible says, "When the fullness of the time had come, God sent forth His Son, born of a woman, born under the law..." (Galatians 4:4)

God knew when to send His Son because He knew the spiritual timing. He knew the harvest of His giving before He gave His Son. As a result, God reaped a family that is made up of millions and millions of people. That is the power of a seed sown at the right time and in the right season.

There are different levels of giving in the Bible. There is the tithe, offerings, alms, blessing someone from your abundance, etc. Again, there is a type of giving that will take you from one financial season to another. That type is sowing a sacrificial seed by faith when God tells you, to whom He tells you, and how much He tells you. It can be given out of your lack or even when you do not have anything.

I can relate with Jacob, who made a faith promise to tithe when he did not have any material possessions (Genesis 28:22). When I made the faith commitment to support that missionary with 10 rupees, it unlocked financial miracles in my life. Jacob became wealthy and had an abundance of material blessings. Each season requires a new level of sacrifice and a new level of faith.

WHY DON'T ALL TITHE-GIVING BELIEVERS PROSPER FINANCIALLY?

You might have asked this question to yourself if you faithfully tithe to your church or organization. I have seen people struggle and sometimes go broke financially though they were giving their tithes and offerings to other ministries. I wondered and asked God why this happens. He opened my understanding and showed me that giving the tithe alone will not bring any financial miracle.

First of all, you need to be a consistent giver in order to reap consistently. If you give occasionally, you will reap occasionally. Secondly, people think that once they pay their tithe they need to wait around for money to show up at their front door or be dropped on their lap by an angel. In the Bible, we do not see anyone receive a financial miracle because they paid their tithes. Abraham was a rich man before he started paying tithes. The Bible does not teach any of those things. Most Christians use Malachi 3:10-11 as their key verses:

"Bring all the tithes into the storehouse, that there may be food in My house, and try Me now in this," says the Lord of hosts, "If I will not open for you the windows of heaven and pour out for you such blessing that there will not be room enough to receive it. And I will rebuke the devourer for your sakes, so that he will not destroy the fruit of your ground, nor shall the vine fail to bear fruit for you in the field," says the Lord of hosts."

They will say God promised that He would open the windows of heaven and pour out blessings that there would not be enough room to contain. Most do not know what type of blessings this verse is talking about. It is not talking about money or material stuff. We do not read anywhere in the Bible or in the history of the Church that God poured out money or cars or houses or any material blessings (He gave manna, but that was not the result of anyone paying a tithe), upon anyone that there was not enough room to contain.

This particular verse is talking about ideas, insight, wisdom, favor, protection, productivity, and opportunities that God will pour out from heaven and we need to put them to work or make use of them to prosper financially. He said He will rebuke the devourer so that he will not destroy the fruit of our ground.

What is a devourer? In the Old Testament time the main source of income and most people's wealth was agriculture. One of the main enemies of farmers was locusts. Locusts devour the crops and leave nothing behind for the harvest. Here, God says He will rebuke the devourer, which means He will rebuke the locusts and other insects that destroy the fruit of the ground.

If there is to be fruit on the ground we need to work hard to produce that fruit. God did not say He will produce the fruit miraculously. We have to work hard and, when the fruit is produced, God will protect it from the enemy and will give us an abundant harvest.

Many believers pay their tithe and God gives them an idea or opportunity, but they will not step out to do it. They will still wait and pray to God for a financial miracle but they are not willing to put their hands to work.

It is like the story of the man who was drowning in a river. He had great faith that God would rescue him. First, a helicopter came and lowered the rope and he denied it, saying that he was waiting on God to save his life. He did not believe that God would utilize natural means to save him. Then a friend came by in a boat and asked him to get into the boat. He denied that also and said, "I am waiting on God to rescue me." He would not swim either, thinking God was big enough to save him from any trouble.

Finally, a sudden surge of flood water came and wiped him away and he died and went to heaven. He was so upset and asked Jesus why He did not come to rescue him when he was drowning. Jesus very lovingly talked to him and said, "First I sent a helicopter to save you and you did not respond. Then I sent your friend in a boat and you still denied his help. You knew how to swim and you could have helped yourself." The poor guy did not know what to say.

There is another powerful scripture in the Bible that talks about giving and its blessings. Proverbs 3:9-10 says, "Honor the Lord with your possessions, and with the first fruits of all your increase; so your barns will be filled with plenty, and your vats will overflow with new wine."

When we honor the Lord with our possessions and first fruits, He has promised that He will bless our barns with plenty. That also shows He will bless the work of our hands. We have to have a barn that is used for collecting the harvest. We have to prepare the land, sow the seeds, protect it from enemies, and wait, and when it is time, God will give us a bountiful harvest.

Vats are the places where the grapes are brought to make wine. We do our part by bringing the grapes and God will bless the work of our hands and give us a harvest that is more than we expected. We should never wait around for a miracle. We should be faithful and work hard with what we have and God will entrust us with more.

In the New Testament Jesus changed the standard of giving and went one step further. In the Old Testament God was in charge of giving us the harvest. We could work hard and do everything we could but from the beginning to the end God was in control of the seed and the harvest. He is the one who gave the rain, rebuked the devourer, etc.

In the New Testament Jesus took the responsibility from God and put it on us to decide how much we are willing to give and how much harvest we should reap. In His teachings to His disciples about changing the mindset from the Old to the New Testament (from the Law to Grace),

He taught about giving in addition to prayer, forgiveness, adultery, etc. He said, "Give, and you will receive. Your gift will return to you in full—pressed down, shaken together to make room for more, running over, and poured into your lap. The amount you give will determine the amount you get back." (Luke 6:38) (NLT)

I used to fast and pray for a financial miracle but it did not come as I expected it to come. I read the above scripture many times but I never understood the depth of it until recently. The last part of the scripture says, "The amount you give will determine the amount you get back." When I understood the meaning, it really opened my eyes. It's no longer God who decides the size of my giving or my harvest, but I get to decide.

Though Jesus talked about tithing in the Gospels, He was talking about it to the Pharisees who were following the law during that time. He never commanded the disciples to continue the Old Testament principle (Matthew 23:23; Luke 11:42). Instead, He let us decide how much we should give, and based on our giving we will reap a harvest.

Paul continued this teaching in his epistles to the churches. He said, "But this I say: He who sows sparingly will also reap sparingly, and he who sows bountifully will also reap bountifully. So let each one give as he purposes in his heart, not grudgingly or of necessity; for God loves a cheerful giver." (2 Corinthians 9:6-7)

If we give ten percent then God will multiply that to thirty, sixty or a hundredfold and give it back to us. If we give twenty percent it will be multiplied back to us. There is no limit except what we decide. I believe a believer in Christ should give at least ten percent and the first fruit of all his increase. The only part God does now is to provide us with the seeds and multiply the seed we have sown.

> "Now may He who supplies seed to the sower, and bread for food, supply and multiply the seed you have sown and increase the fruits of your righteousness." (2 Corinthians 9:10)

Every blessing we receive is a harvest of seeds we have sown. Every farmer, when he harvests his crops, will separate some seeds to sow in the next season. When we receive a blessing from God we must be sure to separate a portion and bless someone else. This book is not about financial breakthrough. If you would like to know more about this subject, please read my soon to be published book, *Why All Tithe Paying Believers Do Not Receive Financial Abundance.*

Chapter 9

THE ENEMY AND GOD'S TIMING
PART 1

"Be sober, be vigilant; because your adversary the devil walks about like a roaring lion, seeking whom he may devour." 1 Peter 5:8

B ELIEVE IT OR NOT, WE HAVE A SPIRITUAL ENEMY WHO IS CON-STANTLY LOOKING FOR OPPORTUNITIES TO SIDETRACK US FROM THE PATH GOD HAS ORDAINED FOR US. One of the advantages the enemy has over us is that he is an invisible enemy. That makes him smarter than us in some ways and he has much more experience in dealing with humans.

If we are to fulfill God's purpose and avoid pitfalls, we need to know how to recognize the enemy's plots as we learn to recognize God's timing. Recognizing his schemes helps us to avoid the major mistakes that great men and women have made throughout history.

We know from the Bible and from experience that the enemy attacks us at very strategic moments; either when we are at a point of great breakthrough, or when we are leisurely enjoying God's blessings. **This is the sixth sign by which we recognize God's timing for our lives.** The enemy is after us to inflict us with whatever brings the greatest damage. His intention is to cause us to miss God's seasons for our lives so we will not fulfill God's purpose for our lives. If we do not fulfill God's purpose concerning our lives it can affect generations after us. The only way the devil will defeat a New Testament believer is through ignorance (2 Corinthians 2:11). Usually, the enemy comes when we are about to enter into a new season in the spirit, so we need to recognize that and be prepared to face him.

There are nine reasons why God allows enemies in our lives:

- An enemy reveals our weaknesses as well as strengths
- Overcoming the enemy brings promotion in the spirit
- An enemy helps us to learn spiritual warfare
- An enemy helps us to recognize God's timing
- An enemy forces us to have spiritual boundaries
- Enemies help us to realize the power and authority of the Word of God
- Enemies present opportunities to exercise self-control
- Enemies remind us of the sovereignty of God
- Enemies cause us to walk in spiritual authority

There are five strategies the enemy generally uses to hinder us from fulfilling God's purpose concerning our lives.

1) DAMAGE, DEFECT, OR DESTROY US IN OUR EARLY YEARS SO WHEN WE ARE GROWN UP WE WILL EITHER NOT BE AROUND, OR WILL DISQUALIFY OURSELVES FROM THE PURPOSE OF GOD.

There are various methods and tools he uses to damage, defect, or destroy us when we are in our childhood. Parents, government, religious background, abuse, and other circumstances are often used by the enemy to damage, defect, or destroy God's people. How and when a baby is conceived and what the mother goes through emotionally has a big impact on the emotional well-being of a baby.

He may use abuse (physical, emotional, or sexual), by people in authority to damage us emotionally so that we will grow up with a wounded soul. Adults who were raised in any kind of abusive situation will feel as if they are missing something or that something is permanently wrong with them.

Physical defects are another tool the enemy uses to keep human beings out of God's will. Many are defected at birth. They come into this earth not fully prepared to cope with life's situations. These can be sicknesses, physical handicaps, or the result of human errors.

Destruction is caused by disregard for human lives. Millions of children were killed throughout history by political, religious, and military leaders. Even today, thousands are being slaughtered every year around the world for the sake of convenience, freedom of choice, wars, and communal fighting.

The Bible contains numerous examples of how the enemy used all of the above tools to prevent some of God's chosen people from being able to accomplish the task for which they were created. When it was time for Moses to be born, the king of Egypt had already released a verdict saying all male children were to be put to death. In the Old Testament, though he worked behind the scenes most of the time, the enemy's works are so vivid in the lives of the people.

The Bible says the enemy comes to steal, kill, and destroy (John 10:10). God always prepares a way of escape for us to survive these onslaughts from the enemy. Otherwise, none of us would be alive to do anything for God.

It is interesting to hear the responses from some of the people whom God chose to use. Many times they tried to talk themselves out of it thinking they were not qualified to be used of God. Gideon, Jeremiah, Moses, Solomon, and King Saul are some of the examples of people who thought they were not qualified to do the job.

It is because of the upbringing they had. They had an insecure feeling about themselves. They may not have received love, acceptance, and appreciation from their parents while they were growing up.

When Jesus was born, the enemy used the government and the religious system of the day to try to destroy Him. He escaped all of the enemy's attacks through God's wisdom and by the power of the Holy Spirit.

2) THWART GOD'S TIMING CONCERNING OUR LIVES IN STRATEGIC MOMENTS BY INFLUENCING US TO MAKE ALTERNATIVE CHOICES SO THAT WE WILL NOT LIVE IN GOD'S PERFECT WILL.

The enemy has long-term and short-term plans against our lives. He somehow recognizes God's timing for our lives and comes to tempt us in the most subtle forms. He knows that if he can influence us to make poor choices he can keep us out of God's perfect will, especially in the areas of life-altering or permanent decisions.

There are four major ways the enemy attacks us to thwart us from walking in God's timing.

A) TEMPTATIONS USING THE LUST OF THE FLESH, LUST OF THE EYE, AND THE PRIDE OF LIFE ARE AMONG HIS MOST COMMON STRATEGIES AGAINST HUMAN BEINGS.

When Jesus finished His forty days of fasting and was getting ready to enter the ministry for which He came to this earth, Satan came to Him with an easy but beguiled plan to keep Him out of God's perfect will.

Imagine that. Jesus was about to begin His public ministry and the enemy recognized that timing and came with an alternative plan. It was an easier road than the path His Father had prepared for Him and he presented the option as if it would accomplish the same goals. Jesus recognized it and resisted him with the Word of God.

Jesus was tempted in the areas of the lust of the flesh (cause the stones to become bread), lust of the eye (he showed Him all the kingdoms of the earth and asked Him to worship him), and the pride of life (he asked Him to jump from the pinnacle of the temple and cause the angels to uphold Him).

> "Now when the devil had ended every temptation, he depart-
> ed from Him until an opportune time." (Luke 4:13)

The Bible says he left Him for a while for a more opportune time. Still, everything that goes wrong in our lives is not an attack from the enemy. Many people perceive it like that and spend a lot of their energy fighting enemies that do not exist. There are some things that happen because we are living in a fallen world.

We may catch a cold because of the weather patterns. We may forget certain things because we have a human brain, or we might be tempted to do certain things because we are living in these earthly bodies. We may get angry at people, which is not necessarily sin or the enemy but if our anger gets out of control it will give the enemy an opportunity to attack us (Ephesians 4:26).

The enemy comes when we are about to step into our divine destinies or when we are about to make a major life decision. Whenever there is a key moment in life, he comes to attack us. When he comes, he does not come as an evil intruder. He will come as an innocent person and appear as an angel of light. It takes a lot of patience and discernment to differentiate his works from what may appear evil. His works may not look evil in the beginning.

B) HE ATTACKS US THROUGH PEOPLE WHO ARE CLOSE TO US OR AROUND US.

Most of the attacks we face on this earth are the enemy using other people; associates, relatives, or even strangers to influence us to make the wrong choice and keep us out of God's perfect will.

Adam and Eve's experience is a perfect example of this tyranny. They were blessed by God in every way we can imagine but the enemy came to Eve and tempted her. She fell for the temptation and ate the fruit God said not to eat, and then gave it to her husband.

The enemy looks for the most vulnerable and sensitive time to attack us. He will bring offenses, hurt, and emotional wounds to prevent or delay us from walking in God's timing.

Jesus was about to finish His earthly ministry and step into His next mission on this earth, which was His crucifixion in Jerusalem. The enemy came through Peter to discourage Him and keep Him out of God's plan. Peter was one of Jesus' closest disciples. The enemy knew Jesus listened to Peter because of the intimacy he had with Him.

When Jesus expressed His plan to go to Jerusalem and that he would be killed by the High Priest and the people, Peter took Him aside and told Him that it should not happen. He tried to tell Jesus that He did not come to earth to die on the cross but to liberate the Jews from Roman power and establish a kingdom for Israel.

Mark 8:31-33 says,

> "And He began to teach them that the Son of Man must suffer many things, and be rejected by the elders and chief priests and scribes, and be killed, and after three days rise again. He spoke this word openly. Then Peter took Him aside and began to rebuke Him. But when He had turned around and looked at His disciples, He rebuked Peter, saying, "Get behind Me, Satan! For you are not mindful of the things of God, but the things of men."

Abraham's example is useful to show the enemy using someone close to him to influence him to step out of God's will. God promised Abraham and Sarah a son. They waited for a while but they did not see any sign of the fulfillment of the promise. Sarah had an idea in her heart to give her maid Hagar to Abraham to have a child by her.

The whole plan was not of God and they (and the whole world) had to pay a heavy price for the choice they made. We are more vulnerable when people who are close to us speak into our lives to do things that may look innocent.

When the Israelites crossed the Jordan River under the leadership of Joshua, God gave them victory over Jericho and they were all encouraged by the great deliverance He had given to them. But, their jubilation did not last long. When they went to attack Ai, they were defeated and had to run for their lives.

God had specifically told them not to take any gold, silver, or precious materials when they captured Jericho. It was the first fruit of their conquest and it belonged to God. But Achan, one of the Israelites, took some of the precious articles and hid them in his tent.

One man's disobedience caused the entire nation to be defeated and 36 people lost their lives in the battle. It is very important that we pray for people who are close to us, or work with us or for us. The enemy can use them at any time to bring damage to us unexpectedly.

C) IGNORANCE IS ANOTHER MAJOR TOOL THE ENEMY USES TO THWART GOD'S TIMING FOR OUR LIVES.

Ignorance of God's Word, ignorance of how the natural world operates, ignorance about family life, finances, leadership, or administration are some of the areas where he tries to keep God's people vulnerable.

The Bible places a great deal of importance on knowledge and wisdom. We need both natural knowledge and revelation knowledge to be successful on this earth. Natural knowledge, or intellectual knowledge, comes through education and experience and is of the mind. Revelation knowledge comes from the Word of God through the inspiration of the Holy Spirit and it is of the spirit.

People in the world have a lot of intellectual knowledge and they are smart in what they do, but worldly intellect has a limit. They perish and go to hell. They lack revelation knowledge that can only be received through the Holy Spirit by a born-again spirit.

On the other hand, I have seen believers and ministers who have a lot of revelation knowledge but are totally deprived of intellectual knowledge and are not effective in the Kingdom. We need both intellectual and revelation knowledge.

We can reach heaven with our revelation knowledge, but we will not be effective on this earth unless we learn how things on this earth work. Jesus said that the children of the world are smarter than the children of the light.

> "Yes, worldly people are smarter with their own kind than spiritual people are." (NCV) (Luke 16:8b)

The Bible says God's people are perishing for lack of knowledge (Hosea 4:6). One thing we lack today in the Christian world is not money, but divine wisdom and strategy. If we reject knowledge, God will reject us from being His servants.

Isaiah 5:13 says,

> "Therefore my people have gone into captivity, because they have no knowledge; their honorable men are famished, and their multitude dried up with thirst."

Another way the enemy keeps people in bondage through ignorance is to deceive them to believe that he does not exist. Or, he deceives people to blame God for what were actually works of the enemy. He is happy whenever he can keep us ignorant in any area of life. There are only two things we need on this earth; wisdom and patience. When we have patience we will be perfect, complete and lack nothing (James 1:4).

D) Deceptions, lies, and half-truths are other ways the enemy works in people's lives to keep them out of God's timing.

The enemy uses our ignorance to deceive us. He speaks lies but portrays them to be truths. He is an expert in speaking lies and Jesus said he is the father of lies. One of the ways he comes to us is as the angel of light who twists the Word of God with half-truths.

Every religion on earth has traces of truth in it, but not the whole truth. Faith in a god, salvation, life after death, and heaven and hell are some of the basic beliefs of most religions. Islam says an angel appeared to Muhammad and gave him the revelation that has become the Koran. There are traces of truth in the Koran but the enemy twisted it and added lies to it.

If you look back in your life at some of the mistakes you made, you will find that you made them because you did not know everything you thought you knew. We need to ask God to fill us with the spirit of wisdom and revelation to expose the lies of the enemy in our lives.

3) INSTIGATE US TO ACT AHEAD OF GOD'S TIMING AND DELAY OR DESTROY GOD'S PLAN CONCERNING OUR LIVES.

One of the things we need to guard against if we are to fulfill God's purpose concerning our lives is impatience. The enemy and the flesh will make us feel that we are running out of time or that our time has passed.

As we have been learning, each one of God's purposes has a specific timing. We do not need to make it happen. All we need to do is hear God's voice and move with Him. This takes a lot of patience, waiting to hear God's voice, and a great deal of walking in the spirit. Patience is a quality of the inner spirit. Our flesh hates patience.

We not only need faith but patience to obtain the promises of God. Hebrews 6:12 says,

> "That you do not become sluggish, but imitate those who through faith and patience inherit the promises."

This book is about how to recognize God's timing for your life. Once we hear from God, the next thing we need to ask Him is about His timing for fulfilling that word. There are many examples in the Bible of people who stepped out in front of God's timing and delayed the fulfillment of their promise for many years.

We are not alone in this race. Many mighty men in the Bible stepped ahead of God's timing to fulfill the purpose He had for them; they failed at first and went through great trials as a result.

Moses is one of the best examples of this. God told Abraham that his children would be in captivity in a foreign land for 400 years. Then He promised He would bring them out of that country with great substance (Genesis 15:13). God orchestrated the whole plan and appointed Moses to bring them out of Egypt.

God put the dream in Moses' heart to be the deliverer of His people, but he did not recognize God's timing for his life. In his zeal and youthfulness he killed an Egyptian and tried to communicate the message to his people that he was going to be their deliverer. The Israelites did not receive him as their judge or deliverer (Exodus 2:11-14).

It was not God's time for them to come out of Egypt because He said they would be in Egypt for 400 years. Moses had to flee from Egypt and go to the wilderness for the next 40 years (Exodus 2:15). Actually, his impatience delayed their deliverance for another 30 years.

How do I know that? The Bible says the Israelites did not leave Egypt until 430 years had passed (Exodus 12:40-41). God said in Genesis that they would leave Egypt after 400 years. Moses' impatience delayed God's purpose concerning his life for 30 years. God is merciful and long-suffering and willing to forgive. When we step out of God's timing, instead of speeding up the process, we delay it.

We could destroy many lives if we try to speed up God's purpose. It is like trying to speed up the process of birthing a baby. Normally, it takes nine months from the conception of a baby until its birth. If we try to speed up the process, we will damage both the baby and the mother.

Another example is the life of Jacob. His mother Rebekah could not have children so Isaac pleaded with the Lord and the Lord granted his request (Genesis 25:21). Rebekah conceived and bore twins. God gave her a prophetic word concerning her children.

Genesis 25:23 says,

> "And the Lord said to her: "Two nations are in your womb, two peoples shall be separated from your body; one people shall be stronger than the other, and the older shall serve the younger."

The older son, Esau, came out first and then Jacob. But Jacob was holding Esau's foot when he came out of the womb (Genesis 25:25-26). The prophecy was that Esau would serve Jacob. Jacob could not wait for the prophecy to be fulfilled. He took advantage of his brother and bought the birthright from him. God will not ask us to deceive or manipulate anyone to fulfill His purpose concerning our lives.

Later, he deceived his father by listening to his mother and stole the blessing from his brother, resulting in a family rivalry. Esau hated his brother and wanted to kill him. Jacob had to flee from his home and lived with his uncle for the next 14 years.

If God has spoken concerning our lives, He is well able to fulfill that word in His time. We do not need to lie and cheat anyone to fulfill God's Word. If we try to do so, we will delay God's purpose concerning our lives.

Another sad story we read is about the children of Aaron who offered incense before the LORD when they were not supposed to. Fire came down from heaven and devoured them and they died instantly. Leviticus 10:1-2 says, "Then Nadab and Abihu, the sons of Aaron, each took his censer and put fire in it, put incense on it, and offered profane fire before the Lord, which He had not commanded them. So fire went out from the Lord and devoured them, and they died before the Lord."

Do not worry and get impatient, thinking your time is running out. When it is the right time God will fulfill His Word concerning your life. There will be no delay, unless we delay it through our own impatience.

Ezekiel 12:25 says,

> "But I, the Lord, will speak. What I say will be done, and it will not be delayed..." (NCV)

Isaiah 55:11 says,

> "So shall My word be that goes forth from My mouth; it shall not return to Me void, but it shall accomplish what I please, and it shall prosper in the thing for which I sent it."

2 Corinthians 1:20 says,

> "For all the promises of God in Him are Yes, and in Him

Amen, to the glory of God through us."

4) ATTACK US WHEN WE ARE SUCCESSFUL AND BRING THE GREATEST DAMAGE TO US AND AS MANY PEOPLE AROUND US AS POSSIBLE.

If the enemy could not do much damage to people while they were children or youths, he lurks until they reach the height of their success and then comes to deceive and to attack them. We have heard and read so many sad stories of great men and women throughout history who made poor choices and destroyed their lives and the lives of others while they were successful.

It is easy to become prideful when we are successful. The enemy will take advantage of our pride and blind us from our weaknesses. We may realize our pride only after we fall or make mistakes.

David is one of the most famous characters in the Bible, let alone the world. He was one of the most renowned kings on this earth, but his life is not excluded from being marred with sin.

There are two major incidents in the Bible when the enemy influenced David to make wrong choices. One was to take a census of the people in his kingdom. He did it without God's counsel and ended up paying a great price, including the death of seventy thousand innocent people who did no wrong but were punished for the sin he committed (1 Chronicles 21:1-30).

> "Now Satan stood up against Israel, and moved David to number Israel. So David said to Joab and to the leaders of the people, "Go, number Israel from Beersheba to Dan, and bring the number of them to me that I may know it." (1 Chronicles 21:1-2)

The second occurrence came during the season when the kings went to war, but David stayed in his palace and saw a woman taking a bath. He was tempted by her and committed adultery with her. She became pregnant and, to cover the shame, he plotted and killed her husband. If we are not careful, when we are successful the enemy will bring us down no matter how important we may be (2 Samuel 11:1-26).

Uzziah was one of the kings of Judah and had a very humble beginning. He became king at the age of sixteen and God blessed whatever he did. He became mighty and famous and, in the end, he also became very prideful.

> "...His fame spread as far as the entrance of Egypt, for he became exceedingly strong." (2 Chronicles 26:8b)

> "But when he was strong his heart was lifted up, to his destruction, for he transgressed against the Lord his God by entering the temple of the Lord to burn incense on the altar of incense." (2 Chronicles 26:16)

Uzziah did not listen to the priest in the temple and was struck with leprosy on his forehead for the rest of his life.

If you want to recognize and live your life according to God's timing, you need to acknowledge that you have an enemy and that he hates you with all that he is. He is not at all excited when you decide to become serious about the purpose of God concerning your life. He lurks at every major turning point in your life and has set well-organized traps.

Those who do not fear God will surely fall into those traps and end their lives in tragedy. May the Lord give us wisdom to escape those traps and hide us under his wings so the enemy cannot see us.

> "Moreover, no man knows when his hour will come: As fish are caught in a cruel net or birds are taken in a snare, so men are trapped by evil times that fall unexpectedly upon them." (Ecclesiastes 9:12) (NIV)

The following verses are the prayers of the Psalmist to deliver him from the snares of the enemy.

> "Keep me from the snares they have laid for me, and from the traps of the workers of iniquity." (Psalm 141:9)

> "The proud have hidden a snare for me, and cords; they have spread a net by the wayside; they have set traps for me." (Psalm 140:5)

"Blessed be the Lord, Who has not given us as prey to their teeth. Our soul has escaped as a bird from the snare of the fowlers; the snare is broken, and we have escaped." (Psalm 124:6-7)

The fifth strategy the enemy uses to thwart us from entering and walking in the new season of our life is to present us with an alternative *opportunity* which will seem an easier and more appealing choice to make. When we look back over our lives we will find that we have made more mistakes by falling prey to this trap than any others. God has given me a little more revelation about this particular strategy of the enemy than the others and I have dedicated the next chapter to it.

Chapter 10

THE ENEMY AND GOD'S TIMING PART 2

"There is a way that seems right to a man, but its end is the way of death."

Proverbs 14:12

AS WE PROGRESS IN OUR WALK WITH GOD ON THIS EARTH, ONE THING WE NEED TO LEARN IS TO DISCERN GOD'S PERFECT WILL AND PERMISSIVE WILL. It is important to know that He has only *one* perfect will concerning an aspect of our life and *many* permissive wills. One of the ways the enemy gets us side-tracked from God's perfect will is through placing good opportunities in front of us when we are at the crossroads of major decisions. Those opportunities will be so alluring that they will almost look like God's perfect will, but only when you step into it and live for a while will you understand the pitfalls. It will always end in pain and regret.

What made Adam and Eve commit sin in the beginning was an opportunity. The devil presented an opportunity to Adam and Eve to become like God. They thought that was an excellent idea and it did not look dangerous to eat the fruit. It was attractive, appealing, and approving to the natural mind. I have made choices in my life based on opportunity and I always ended up losing in the end. We are here for a purpose and of course we need opportunities to fulfill our destiny, but, all opportunities are not sent by God. If you are not sure the opportunity you have is sent by God to help you fulfill your destiny, never accept it.

Joseph had a powerful dream about becoming someone of great importance. On his way to fulfilling that dream he was tempted with an opportunity to sleep with his master's wife. He chose his destiny over that opportunity and was spared from great troubles.

Abraham was given a promise to be the father of multitudes. He was a man of destiny. His wife presented him with an opportunity to fulfill that promise by having a child by their maidservant. He failed to recognize that it was an opportunity from the enemy to delay the plan of God. He accepted the opportunity and had a son by Hagar. Even today the whole world is facing the consequence of that one wrong decision.

Several years ago, we were pastoring a church on the East Coast that was thriving in the beginning. All of a sudden we entered a season where the people were no longer as excited about the church and the vision as they used to be. The honeymoon was over for us as pastors and for the believers in their new church and now it was time to take hold of the Word that God gave us; to persevere in the Spirit and plow through.

We did not have the maturity in the spirit to do that and we thought it was time to move to our next assignment. Some of the key people whom I thought would be leaders left the church. I was really discouraged and did not know what to do. It does not matter what you do in your life, there will come a time when you lose your initial excitement and it requires much maturity and perseverance to continue.

I believe the devil also knew this and I went for a ministry trip to the Midwest where we have many good friends. While I was there, I met a precious man who was starting a new ministry. He approached me and asked if I could run an area of his ministry. He took me to a brand new 1.5 million dollar house and took me inside. No one else had ever lived there. The builders had just finished the house. He told me that I could move into that house any time I wanted and stay as long as I want for free.

Everything looked so attractive and I called my wife and explained to her about the house and the opportunity. Nothing could have looked more attractive, alluring and more timely. Without thinking much, we decided to leave the church and move. They even sent a person to drive our personal belongings and paid for the moving. We moved in and started to do the ministry there. But, as the Bible says, "There is a way that seems perfect to man but it will be a way of death at the end." (Proverbs 14:12)

Storms came against our lives and ministry and we went through the most painful experience of our lives. God rescued us from that, although it took more than two years to recover from the pain and the wounds incurred from that experience. We should not have moved from the East Coast just because we were going through difficulties or because we had an alluring opportunity. We should have waited to hear God's voice and direction. Thankfully, God is a God of restoration and all things worked together for our good at the end.

There are many characters in the Bible who chose opportunity over their destiny and destroyed their lives. Esau chose a bowl of stew to satisfy his appetite. He sold his birthright and was rejected by God. Some of the saddest people in the Bible I can think of are Lot, Esau, Balaam, and Gehazi. These four people had a mighty destiny to fulfill. Instead, they were attracted by an opportunity and shipwrecked their lives.

Lot was Abraham's nephew who traveled with him to the land of Canaan. They both were very rich but strife broke out between their servants. They separated from each other and Lot saw that the land of Sodom and Gomorrah was prosperous and provided great opportunity to feed his sheep and become exceedingly wealthy. But, the people living in those cities were exceedingly wicked before God and He decided to destroy them.

God rescued Lot and his family, but his wife became a pillar of salt. His daughters committed incest with him and brought forth two nations, the Moabites and Ammonites, which were cursed by God. Sometimes opportunities can cost us our lives if they are not sent by God.

Balaam was a diviner from the land of Pethor (Numbers 22:5) who was called by Balak the king of Moab to pronounce curses over Israel. The king sent his messengers with great gifts to call Balaam but God spoke to him that night not to go with them. Unfortunately, he was so enamored by the invitation that he finally went in the permissive will of God. He was nearly killed on the way by an angel but his donkey saved him (Numbers 22:31-34). He went to Balak but God put blessings in his mouth to bless Israel instead of cursing them.

Balak became upset and was angry at Balaam. He told him how much he was planning to honor Balaam if he had cursed Israel (Numbers 24:10). Finally, he said, "Now therefore, flee to your place. I said I would greatly honor you, but in fact, the Lord has kept you back from honor" (Numbers 24:11). If he had accepted the honor from Balak and cursed Israel, that would have been the end of his life.

Gehazi was the servant of the prophet Elisha. Naaman, the captain of the army of Syria, was a leper. He came to know that if he went to see Elisha he could receive his healing. So, the king of Syria sent a letter and servants loaded with great gifts and materials to bless Elisha (2 Kings 5:5). He came to Elisha and Elisha ordered him to go and dip himself in the Jordan seven times to be healed. He obeyed the prophet and was healed of his leprosy.

He came to Elisha and offered all the gifts he brought but Elisha rejected everything. Gehazi, who would have been the successor of Elisha, became greedy and saw a once-in-a-lifetime opportunity to become rich. He valued natural wealth more than the anointing that he was going to inherit.

Naaman and his servants left Elisha, but Gehazi ran after them. He lied to them and received their gifts. He brought them home and stored them in his house. Then he came and stood before the prophet as if nothing had occurred. The man of God saw all this in his spirit and caught Gehazi red-handed (2 Kings 5:20-26).

Gehazi was cursed with the leprosy of Naaman and lost everything, including his destiny. It was not only Gehazi who was affected by this act but also the generations after him. This is the way generational curses begin and operate. Elisha said, "Therefore the leprosy of Naaman shall cling to you and your descendants forever. "And he (Gehazi) went out from his presence leprous, as white as snow." (2 Kings 5:27)

Shortcuts to become rich, fleshly satisfaction, or fame will always look attractive in the beginning and many are falling into this trap these days. May the Lord protect us from the traps of opportunities that are not of God.

God taught me the following differences between following opportunity and following destiny. I believe there are two kinds of opportunities: one will satisfy the flesh, which will always bring pain at the end, and one is of the spirit and is part of our destiny. We need to know how to discern between these two. I believe the following points will help us do that. The Bible says, "There is a way that seems right to a man, but its end is the way of death." (Proverbs 16:25)

1) Opportunity is a trap that slowly takes us away from God

I have seen many precious men and women who prayed for a great while for an open door and suddenly there appeared before them the opportunity of a lifetime. They did not wait to ask God whether they should accept it or not, but rather jumped and started a business, a new venture or a relationship. Slowly, it began to engulf them and take all of their time until finally; they had no time for anything else.

The very thing they thought would bring them joy and draw them closer to God and be a help to the Kingdom of God was taking them away from all they thought was important. They did not have time for family or God. Days and months would pass before they even had time to pray or read the Bible. Life was like sailing away in a boat on the ocean. The farther away from the shore they went, the more lost they felt. Finally, these people would end up broke and broken in every way and deeply wounded. It is not easy to restore these people because this process occurs gradually over a period of time.

DESTINY DRAWS YOU CLOSER TO GOD

You cannot fulfill your destiny without God. Your destiny began in God and was birthed by Him. You need His direction and companionship to fulfill your destiny. The closer you walk with God, the more pages of your destiny will unfold. The more time you spend with Him, the higher you go in your life. Destiny is less effort with greater results. Opportunity is more work with fewer results. Whatever you start by the guidance of the Holy Spirit will always draw you closer to God and not take you away from Him.

2) OPPORTUNITY IS SELF-FOCUSED

Many opportunities come and knock at our door and say the same thing. "Look, here is a way you can get rich quickly. You can be very successful and you will earn the respect of your friends and family. No one else has ever had such an opportunity before. This is one of a kind and comes once in a lifetime. You can become prominent and rich enough to be able to help a lot of other people and also the Kingdom of God." Does this sound familiar to you? Do not look in that direction because many have fallen prey to those slogans.

DESTINY IS GOD-FOCUSED

Destiny comes and knocks at your door and says, "It will be hard in the beginning. You will need a lot of perseverance and patience to keep going. But, at the end everything will work out well. You need to depend on God for your every move. Troubles and storms will come your way but be strong because many have gone before you and reached their goals. Wealth and popularity are secondary; being pleasing to God has to be the priority. Do not try to avoid problems or take shortcuts. It will only make things more difficult later."

3) OPPORTUNITY DEPENDS UPON YOUR ABILITY

Opportunity is all about what you can accomplish through your strength, ability, knowledge, and influence. It will require even the last ounce of your energy and the hospital will be the last 'resort' you will ever visit. To fulfill your destiny God has already given you the grace and faith that you need. The Bible says not to lean on our own understanding but to trust God in all our ways (Proverbs 3:5-6).

Destiny depends on God's ability

Destiny is all about what God can do through us. When we go through some hard times, God will be there to comfort and rescue us. That does not mean you will never fall or make any mistakes. Whatever happens, God will be on our side and He will be our strength. We cannot fulfill our destiny by our own strength or ability. It is beyond our ability and only through God can it be accomplished. Each goal is achieved through God and by God.

4) Opportunity creates anxiety

Opportunities are time-oriented and if we do not say yes today, they will not be there tomorrow. Because we rely on ourselves to fulfill them, they always create anxiety, stress, and restlessness in us. There will always be pressure from other people and situations that take away our peace of mind. All of the responsibility and weight is on our shoulders.

Destiny gives you peace

You know the Author and Finisher of your faith is God and He is faithful and trustworthy. You do not need to carry all of the burdens yourself. You can load them on Him. God has promised us peace even in the midst of storms. I have experienced both. I have stepped out to take hold of opportunity and went through all kinds of turmoil in my life. But, I have also had peace in the midst of great storms when I was walking in my destiny.

5) Opportunity is temporary

It is always based on the weather, market, or circumstances. It can be lost or finished over time. I know the old saying, "Opportunities do not wait for us." That is true but we have to know for sure which one is from God. When you are serious about your destiny, even if you miss one opportunity God will send another one.

Destiny is eternal

Destiny is a life-long process that only ends when you take your last breath. It is the purpose of your very existence on this earth. Your destiny began in God and will end in God. You will not retire from your destiny. When you fulfill your destiny, you will leave this earth.

6) Opportunity is always about popularity, influence, and success

It is about how many people will know about us, or how much money it is going to generate. How often will we be able to do it? The numbers, numbers, numbers. That is all that matters with opportunistic people. Destiny focuses on relationship; opportunity focuses on immediate gratification.

Destiny always focuses on glorifying God

Destiny is all about how something glorifies God. How many people will benefit from this? How many people will I be able to bless? Whatever we do, our motive should be to glorify God.

7) Opportunity always promises shortcuts which will bring short-lived luxury, comfort, and self-gratification and produces long-term pain.

Opportunity tells us how wonderful it would be for us, how fulfilling and luxurious. At the end, it will bite us like a poisonous snake. The Bible talks about those who hasten to become rich. They will fall into many temptations. 1 Timothy 6:9 says, "But those who desire to be rich fall into temptation and a snare, and into many foolish and harmful lusts which drown men in destruction and perdition."

Destiny always promises victory, joy in the middle of suffering, and long-term results

Anyone God used mightily on this earth went through trials and struggles. Jesus did not promise us a life without problems, but a victorious and triumphant life over problems. Opportunities are always attractive and pleasing to the flesh. Destiny always bears witness with your spirit and may not be pleasing to the flesh.

Then, the question is, "How do you fulfill your destiny without opportunity?" To fulfill your destiny you do not need to look for opportunities. You need to listen to your Father in heaven and do what He tells you. Jesus did not look for opportunities to minister, but always waited to hear from His Father before He made a move.

Whenever you have to make a choice that is going to affect your destiny, or if the result of your choice is going to remain for the rest of your life, then I would suggest you do not rush it. Please get wise counsel from people (more than one) who are mature. I want to especially tell young people, never ask your peers for advice when you want to make a decision that will affect your destiny. Your peers may not be able to give you wise counsel because they have yet to learn much in their lives. They themselves may not have experienced the results of such decisions.

The Bible says in Proverbs 11:14,

> "Where there is no counsel, the people fall; but in the multitude of counselors there is safety."

Chapter 11

THE NIGHT SEASONS

*"O my God, I cry in the daytime, but You do not hear; and in the **night season**, and am not silent."* Psalm 22:2

*"I will bless the LORD who has given me counsel; my heart also instructs me in the **night seasons**."* Psalm 16:7 (emphasis added)

THE SEVENTH SIGN BY WHICH GOD COMMUNICATES HIS TIMING IS WHEN HE ALLOWS US TO GO THROUGH A SEASON CALLED THE NIGHT SEASON. One powerful revelation that I found from the Word is that whenever God did something major in human history, He did it during the night time or in the dark hours. I believe the reason is since the devil is the god of darkness and his works are done in darkness, God wants to show that He is the Light and that His goodness overrides the power of darkness.

In the book of Genesis, most of creation was brought forth during the night time. Each day after creating, God said, "...Evening and morning were the first day," etc. (Genesis 1:5). Evening is mentioned before the morning. That means there was evening before the morning came. He worked in the evening and ended in the morning. We read that darkness was already upon the face of the deep. God created the light out of darkness. 2 Corinthians 4:6 says, "For God, who commanded the light to shine out of darkness, hath shined in our hearts..." (KJV)

Whenever God does something major in our lives and for our lives, He does it without our support or help. He likes to do it in the 'dark.' Adam was in a deep sleep when God took Eve out of Him. Genesis 2:21 says, "And the Lord God caused a deep sleep to fall on Adam, and he slept; and He took one of his ribs, and closed up the flesh in its place." Creating the woman was a major milestone for life on this earth.

When God made a covenant with Abraham it was in the midst of darkness. Genesis 15:12, 17-18 says, "Now when the sun was going down, a deep sleep fell upon Abram; and behold, horror and great darkness fell upon him... And it came to pass, when the sun went down and it was dark, that behold, there appeared a smoking oven and a burning torch that passed between those pieces. On the same day the Lord made a covenant with Abram..."

When God delivered the people of Israel from Egypt, the last plague of the death of the firstborn took place at midnight. The deliverance actually took place at night and the angel of death visited the homes of the Egyptians at night time. Exodus 12:12 says, "For I will pass through the land of Egypt on that night, and will strike all the firstborn in the land of Egypt, both man and beast; and against all the gods of Egypt I will execute judgment: I am the Lord." Verse 29 says, "And it came to pass at midnight that the Lord struck all the firstborn in the land of Egypt..."

Verse 31 says,

> "Then he [Pharaoh] called for Moses and Aaron by night, and said, "Rise, go out from among my people, both you and the

children of Israel..."

When they came to the Red Sea, the Egyptians followed the Israelites to capture them. God came between them and created darkness to separate His people from the Egyptians and wrought the miracle of parting the Sea (Exodus 14:20).

Some of the significant battles in the Old Testament were won in the night time. Some of the major directions from God were given to people during the night. Job 33:14-16 says, "For God may speak in one way, or in another, yet man does not perceive it. In a dream, in a vision of the night, when deep sleep falls upon men, while slumbering in their beds, then He opens the ears of men, and seals their instruction."

God spoke to Moses on Mount Sinai in the midst of darkness. Exodus 20:21 says, "So the people stood afar off, but Moses drew near the thick darkness where God was."

There is a great chance that Jesus was born at night and there is evidence to support this. One reason is, the Bible says the inn was full and there was no room for Joseph and Mary (Luke 2:7). Travelers stop at night and stay at an inn to sleep. Secondly, the angels went to the shepherds at night to announce His birth (Luke 2:8-9).

When Jesus was on the cross paying the price for our sin, the whole earth was filled with darkness for three hours and it was the most pivotal point in human history. Matthew 27:45 says, "Now from the sixth hour until the ninth hour there was darkness over all the land."

This book would be incomplete if I did not write about the Night Seasons, since this book is about recognizing God's timing. One of the ways God communicates His timing to our lives on this earth is by having us go through the Night Seasons.

In our walk with God on this earth we all will go through a season of life called the "Night Seasons," where you and I feel that we are walking through darkness and we cannot see anything in the future or even what lies in our past. We will feel like God has deserted us and nothing good will ever happen for us again. You may feel that you are shut in on all sides, like God has laid His hand upon you and you cannot move (Psalm 139:5).

Signs you are going through the Night Season:

- If you feel like your dreams will never come true

- If you are lonely and all of your close friends are away from you

- If you are going through great pain emotionally and physically

- If you feel like it is better to be dead than alive

- If you feel as if everything you were holding onto was suddenly taken away from you

- If you lost all excitement about life and whatever you do

- If you feel you are stuck and you cannot move forward or backward in time

- If you feel like God has left you though you tried to obey Him in everything

- If you feel like your vision and dreams are dead and your future looks bleak

The Night Season might be caused by some incident that happened in your life that made you feel like 'everything is over.' It could be a business loss, the loss of a loved one, or betrayal by someone who is close to you. You need to know how to go through this season in order to be victorious in life. There is nothing more difficult on this earth than going through your Night Season. You will experience birth pangs, and you might feel that you are going to have an emotional breakdown.

God sometimes allows the enemy to persecute us for a season just like he did to Job. Jesus told Peter that Satan asked for him to sift him as wheat (Luke 22:31).

God allows us to go through this season but we must understand that major growth and maturity in our spiritual lives is developed during this time. In the natural, when babies grow they eat and sleep more than usual. Trees and flowers prepare their food during the daytime and grow at night time. I have been through this season more than once in my life. I want to tell you that if it was not for the grace of God, I would not be alive today.

David went through this season several times in his life. One was when he had to flee for his life from the palace for fear of King Saul (1 Samuel 19:10; 27:1). Another incident is when the Amalekites came and captured all the women, children, and their substance from Ziklag and burned the city when he and his men were not there. He lost everything in one day; his wives, children, and all the materials he had. The men he had been taking care of turned against him and spoke of stoning him (1 Samuel 30:1-6).

The Bible says David and the men who were with him cried until they had no more power to weep. That is a perfect example of going through the Night Season.

> "Then David and the people who were with him lifted up their voices and wept, until they had no more power to weep."
> (1 Samuel 30:4)

Another instance is when David had to flee for his life while he was the king of Israel. His son Absalom ran a coup and took over the kingdom (2 Samuel 15:13-15).

David said in Psalm 23:4, "Yea, though I walk through the valley of the shadow of death, I will fear no evil; for You are with me; Your rod and Your staff, they comfort me." God is with you during this season and He has prepared some comfort mechanisms (that I will share with you in this chapter), which we need if we are to make it through this season.

The following scriptures describe the state of the soul of a person who is going through this season better than any words I can use.

Psalm 18:4-6 says,

> "The pangs of death surrounded me, and the floods of ungodliness made me afraid. The sorrows of Sheol surrounded me; the snares of death confronted me. In my distress I called upon the Lord, and cried out to my God; He heard my voice from His temple, and my cry came before Him, even to His ears."

Psalm 116:3 says,

> "The pains of death surrounded me, and the pangs of Sheol laid hold of me; I found trouble and sorrow."

Psalm 143:3-4 says,

> "For the enemy has persecuted my soul; He has crushed my life to the ground; He has made me dwell in darkness, like those who have long been dead. Therefore my spirit is overwhelmed within me; my heart within me is distressed."

This is the season of utter hopelessness and weakness and you feel you have come to the end of your life. This season is very important to God because that is when He is busiest working in your life and on your behalf.

Ways God Sustains Us During the Night Seasons

God gives us a song

During the Night Seasons God will put songs in our spirit that will encourage, comfort, and inspire us. There will be particular worship songs that you will like during this time more than any other time before. Job 35:10 says, "But no one says, "Where is God my Maker, who gives songs in the night?" Psalm 42:8 says, "The Lord will command His lovingkindness in the daytime, and in the night His song shall be with me—a prayer to the God of my life." Psalm 77:6 says, "I call to remembrance my song in the night; I meditate within my heart, and my spirit makes diligent search."

When we walk through the valley of the shadow of death, His rod and staff shall comfort us. He will surround us with songs of deliverance. Psalm 32:7 says, "You are my hiding place; You shall preserve me from trouble; You shall surround me with songs of deliverance." When you sing the songs God brings to your heart, they will bring comfort and deliverance to your life.

We will cry more than usual

Crying is one of the ways we release our pain and emotional stress. Psalm

6:6 says, "I am weary with my groaning; all night I make my bed swim; I drench my couch with my tears." Here the Psalmist is going through some painful experiences in his own life and he is crying out to God for His help and mercy.

Psalm 42:3 says,

> "My tears have been my food day and night, while they continually say to me, "Where is your God?"

He will reveal some intimate things to us

In the natural, precious metals and stones are hidden in the darkness. They are not visible to the natural eyes. It takes a lot of effort and pain to dig out some of these metals. When we go through the Night Seasons, God will reveal some things about our lives that we would know in no other way. Job 12:22 says, "He [God] uncovers deep things out of darkness, and brings the shadow of death to light." God spoke some intimate things to people in the Bible during their Night Seasons.

God gives special instructions to our heart during the Night Season.

Psalm 16:7 says,

> "I will bless the Lord who has given me counsel; my heart also instructs me in the night seasons."

When we go from one season to another we receive knowledge from God that we did not have before.

Psalm 19:2 says,

> "Day unto day utters speech, and night unto night reveals knowledge."

He fights our enemies at night

There will be times during this season when you will be suddenly awakened from sleep and you will feel that sleep has left you. God is waking you up to pray and intercede, so do not go back to sleep until you pray. Psalm 119:148 says, "My eyes are awake through the night watches, that I may meditate on Your word."

Our God neither sleeps nor slumbers. He is always watching over us. Job 34:24-25 says, "He breaks in pieces mighty men without inquiry, and sets others in their place. Therefore He knows their works; He overthrows them in the night, and they are crushed."

Great deliverances are accomplished during the Night Seasons

God fought for the people of Israel against the Egyptians at night time. Paul and Silas were imprisoned, but at midnight they began to sing praises to God and an earthquake shook the prison so they and all the other prisoners were set free from bondage (Acts 16:25-26).

While the disciples were at sea one night, a great storm came against their boat and it was about to sink. Jesus came to them in the fourth watch of the night and rescued them (Matthew 14:24-32).

He will put an increased hunger in our heart for His Word

God will remind us of His promises to us. Though we may not feel like believing the Word, we need to meditate and speak His Word to our circumstances. Read and meditate on His Word day and night and your deliverance will come.

When we go through the Night Seasons our focus is on the result, but God's focus is on the process. We are looking forward to the reward when God is focusing on how we respond while we are in the process. The process—not the result—is what changes us. We look for the result because we do not like the process.

Psalm 63:6 says,

> "When I remember You on my bed, I meditate on You in the night watches."

God examines our heart at night

Psalm 17:3 says,

> "You have tested my heart; You have visited me in the night; You have tried me and have found nothing; I have purposed that my mouth shall not transgress."

The Night Season is all about our heart. God will test our heart during night seasons and during night time. He tests our attitude in those times when things are not going well for us.

In the above scripture, the Psalmist says he has purposed in his heart that he shall not transgress with his mouth. The flesh wants to scream at God and others when we go through the Night Seasons, but we need to have self-control in what we say because our words have power to alter our destiny.

Chapter 12

TWO KINDS OF SPIRITUAL TIMING

"...Disclose to you the secrets of wisdom,
for true wisdom has two sides." Job 11:6 (NIV)

THERE ARE TWO KINDS OF SPIRITUAL TIMING. You need to know how to identify them in order to move forward with God. Those who are blessed in the Kingdom are those who move in God's timing. The first kind of spiritual timing pertains to promotion in your spirit.

As we expect our children to grow and mature, our heavenly Father wants all of His children to grow up spiritually and become overcomers on this earth. When you are getting ready for a spiritual promotion you will go through circumstances that are really irritable. When we hear spiritual promotion we always look for some tangible blessing. Spiritual promotion means the change and growth that takes place in your heart, spirit and attitude through overcoming negative feelings and circumstances. You will know inwardly something has changed when this takes place.

God wants us to face our circumstances, temptations, and challenges with maturity instead of being victimized by them over and over again. If you are experiencing dissatisfaction, agitation, irritation, trouble, inward commotion, loss of peace of mind, restlessness, feelings of fear and dread, anxiety or distress, it is a sign that God wants you to overcome and mature in those areas. These are strategic moments in the spirit. The enemy knows that very well and he will influence you to react in the flesh so you will not make any progress in your spiritual life. This cycle will continue in our lives as long as we are in this earthly suit. We need to reach a place in our lives where we will praise, serve and do what God says regardless of what and how we feel.

The second kind occurs in the natural realm and includes a change in physical location and/or a tangible promotion. What I mean by change in physical location and promotion is that you move to a new position, town, city or country. Most new seasons in my life have had a new physical location. Sometimes, there was more than one location for the same season. Maybe it is because the ministerial calling on my life requires a lot of traveling.

I am not saying every believer has to move to a new location in every new season of life. This might be applicable only to some who are in five-fold ministry. Many believers may stay at the same place and the same church all their lives and experience their new seasons in the spirit.

If you look at the animal kingdom, some birds and animals migrate from one region to another to avoid changing weather patterns. In the natural, to enter into the new season they have to move to a new location. They move to a place that is more comfortable to find food and to breed. Some birds fly hundreds of miles and go to a different continent every year. It is important to notice that only some birds and animals relocate and there are others that stay in the same place regardless of the weather.

Jeremiah 8:7 says,

> "Even the birds in the sky know the right times to do things. The storks, doves, swifts, and thrushes know when it is time to migrate. But my people don't know what the Lord wants them to do." (NCV)

Jesus had to move to different locations in His life. He was born in Bethlehem and then had to flee to Egypt for His childhood. Then He came back to Nazareth and stayed there until he began His ministry. After He began His ministry He did not go back to Bethlehem or Nazareth, instead He went to Galilee, and then to Capernaum, Bethany, and other places.

Joseph was taken to different places and Moses had the same experience. It is extremely unlikely that you will stay in one place for all the seasons of your life. At the least, God will take you away for training and bring you back to your original place. If you have a ministerial calling on your life it is definite that God will take you to other places before He will use you.

There is something about traveling to different places that develops your maturity and the different skills that you need to fulfill God's call on your life. One of the reasons He takes you to other places is to expose you to His truth and revelations that work in that place. Every city and nation has a different revelation of God's glory and truth and He will take you to the place that best fits your purpose.

I have changed my location 13 times, and 11 of those moves occurred after I entered the ministry. I had to move more than once to finish one season in my life. I am talking about different states and countries, not moving to a different corner of the same town.

When we study the life of Jesus we see that He had a clear understanding about His purpose and the timing of His purpose. He knew that His destiny was the cross. He knew in His spirit about the imminent death awaiting Him in Jerusalem. I can only imagine how the burden of this destiny weighed on Jesus as He took His disciples to the Garden of Gethsemane on the night He was arrested.

What happened to Him there? He began to agonize and be sorrowful. The mental agony was the worst He ever faced in His earthly life. What was he doing in Gethsemane? He was giving birth to His new season and enduring great pain and sorrow.

> "Then He said to them, "My soul is exceedingly sorrowful, even to death. Stay here and watch with Me." (Matthew 26:38)

> "And being in agony, He prayed more earnestly..." (Luke 22:44)

Sometimes when you enter into a new season you may need a change of location. Other times you stay where you are and enter into your new season. Biblical figures like Abraham, Jacob, Joseph, Moses, David, Esther, and Ruth are some examples of people who changed their locations when they entered into a new season in their lives.

Only God can show you how to recognize whether or not a new season in the spirit requires a change of location in the natural. Sometimes you get a spiritual promotion and change of location at the same time. Other times either you get spiritually promoted and continue to stay where you are or you change your location and are not promoted spiritually at that time.

In the Old Testament, when the people of Israel were going through the wilderness they had to make many stops on the way. God sent a pillar of cloud to guide them and the people moved whenever the cloud moved. When the cloud stopped moving, it was a sign for the people to stop and they would stay in that place as long as the cloud remained.

> "And the LORD went before them by day in a pillar of cloud to lead the way, and by night in a pillar of fire to give them light, so as to go by day and night. He did not take away the pillar of cloud by day or the pillar of fire by night from before the people." (Exodus 13:21-22)

> "Whether it was two days, a month, or a year that the cloud remained above the tabernacle, the children of Israel would remain encamped and not journey; but when it was taken up, they would journey." (Numbers 9:22)

The Israelites had to watch the cloud to see when it moved next because as soon as the cloud moved, they had to pack up and leave. That is moving according to spiritual timing. God did not lead them by a natural clock that was made by man. He navigated them according to His timing. In the same way, God may ask you to move from one place to another. You must be able to sense for yourself when the cloud is moving.

If everything is going well in the natural but inside you are not happy and know something needs to happen, it may be the sign of a time of spiritual breakthrough in your life. If you are facing emotional pain, rejection from others, betrayal, and so forth; then this may be a sign that you are getting close to your next spiritual promotion.

Most people interpret these pains as an attack from the devil and step out of God's will and do stupid things. These are great moments in the spirit and have great potential to form or alter your destiny. In these moments of your life you need to give all of your attention to what the Spirit is saying.

When a woman is close to giving birth to a baby she cannot do everything as others do. She has to protect that baby and take good care of herself. She cannot be undisciplined and run around all day long. There is a great discomfort she feels in her physical body. She knows something is about to happen. Oftentimes, trials are the sign of the birth of a new season in your life. The greater the trial; the greater the breakthrough that is awaiting you.

Many people get upset with God when they go through trials in their lives. No one likes pain and we all try desperately to avoid it. When we lose someone we love, or things do not happen the way we want, we can get bitter toward God and ourselves. You may feel all of these things temporarily in your life. As long as you keep your heart tender toward God, everything will be fine at the end.

David was a shepherd boy and his brothers were soldiers in King Saul's army. I believe one of the reasons David was chosen to be the shepherd boy was because his parents and brothers did not think he was strong enough or tall enough to be in an army. He may have gone through much rejection and thought himself insignificant.

One day God spoke to Samuel to go to Jesse's house (David's father) to anoint a new king. Samuel told the family his reason for coming and called everyone for a special dinner. They totally ignored David and did not even consider him important enough to be invited. Samuel asked Jesse, "Are all the young men here?"

Then he said,

> "There remains yet the youngest, and there he is, keeping the sheep." And Samuel said to Jesse, "Send and bring him. For we will not sit down till he comes here." (1 Samuel 16:11)

When Samuel saw the firstborn, he thought surely he was the chosen of the Lord, but God rejected each of them one by one. Finally, Samuel asked if anyone had been left out and they told him there was one more and that he was a shepherd boy. Samuel asked them to call David and, when he came in, God said to anoint him to be the new king of Israel.

> "So he sent and brought him in. Now he was ruddy, with bright eyes, and good looking. And the LORD said, "Arise, anoint him; for this is the one!" (1 Samuel 16:12)

Imagine the emotional struggle David might have gone through, or imagine that you were David and you were not invited for a special family dinner. You would feel hurt, humiliated and rejected. But, that was the beginning of a new season for David.

You may feel like quitting and running away from your problems. That may seem easier but it is not the answer. You may be saying things you should not be saying. I want you to know that God is not upset about anything you say. There is nothing new to Him. He knows it all. But, what He looks for is any sign of repentance. As long as you come back to Him and ask His forgiveness, everything will work together for good.

Elijah was one of the mighty prophets of the Lord in the Old Testament. The Word of the Lord came to him one day and he proclaimed a drought in Israel (1 Kings 17:1). God told him to go to the brook Cherith to hide from the king and said He would command the ravens to feed him (1 Kings 17:3-4).

The prophet was there for a while and then the brook began to dry up.

Soon he did not have any more water to drink. Naturally, he may have thought to himself, "Hey, God sent me here and I am supposed to be here, so then why are these hardships coming my way?" It was a sign for his next move. The Word of the Lord came to him there and instructed him about the next season he was going to enter.

> "Then the word of the LORD came to him, saying, "Arise, go to Zarephath, which belongs to Sidon, and dwell there. See, I have commanded a widow there to provide for you." (1 Kings 17:8-9)

This is another example about how a new season often requires a change of location. Just because God told you to go to a place does not mean it is permanent and you are going to stay there until you die. No, you need to be open to His leading all the time.

Physical problems, adverse circumstances, lack of work, lack of opportunity for your gift to operate, and financial struggles may be signs for you to seek God to see if He is trying to communicate something to you. Even so, unless He gives the order; do not move. Just because you are going through some struggle in your life does not mean you need to relocate to another area. Wait and ask for His direction.

People move to a new place to run away from their problems, only to find that changing locations does not solve those problems. If He speaks in the midst of the pain, then you obey His voice or seek counsel from spiritual leaders who are mature in the things of God. When they give counsel it will either immediately bear witness, or cause you to wait upon God until the counsel is confirmed in your spirit.

When we study the life of Abraham, we see this principle many times. Abram's father, Terah, took his family and his grandson Lot from Ur to go into the land of Canaan and they reached Haran and dwelt there (Genesis 11:31). Terah died in Haran and we can imagine the family suffered terrible pain.

That was the beginning of a new season in Abram's life. After his father died, the Lord appeared to Abram for the first time and gave him promises. Abram started His journey with his family, including his nephew Lot.

Every time he stopped somewhere, something would happen in his life to keep him moving.

Sometimes when things seem to be going well in the natural, you will eventually reach a place where you are deeply dissatisfied in your spirit and you may become sorrowful, frustrated, stressed, unhappy, discouraged, or depressed. This may be a sign of your next season in the spirit.

During each season, God develops our faith and spirit in a new way. It is similar to working out in a gym. There are many different pieces of equipment to develop different muscles in your body. You cannot keep using the same exercise equipment and expect all the muscles in your body to grow strong. You need to find the right kind of equipment that will help you develop a particular muscle.

Everyone wants a healthy body and great looking muscles. But, you know you have to go through great pain to develop those muscles. It is not an easy thing; as you know if you ever tried to work out in a gym. When people see others with a great, muscular body or in good shape, they think, "I wish my body looked like that." Yes, it can, but are you willing to go through the pain they went through to develop their bodies?

It is the same when people see God using someone mightily and wish they had that kind of anointing. Yes, you can, but are you willing to go through some trials and pain to get there?

God will develop each spiritual muscle in your life through different experiences until you become totally mature and lack nothing.

> "That you may walk properly toward those who are outside,
> and that you may lack nothing." (1 Thessalonians 4:12)

Faith has different muscles. The faith you have for a financial miracle is not enough for physical healing because this is another dimension of faith. Some people have great faith for believing things for other people but when they need to believe for themselves they freak out. Some people have great faith to cast out demons but they cannot believe God for a hundred dollars. That does not mean they are not spiritual, but they have not developed that particular faith muscle. They can, and God may have brought circumstances into their lives, but they just would not grasp it and grow up.

No temptation or trial is joyful at the time you are going through it, but, at the end, you will come out good and fit for the work of the Kingdom.

> "Now no chastening seems to be joyful for the present, but painful; nevertheless, afterward it yields the peaceable fruit of righteousness to those who have been trained by it." (Hebrews 12:11)

Naomi and her family fled to Moab in the time of famine, but she did not want to return to Israel. Her sons took Moabite women as their wives, which was not according to God's perfect will. God had to allow some hardships into their lives to get their attention. When she lost her husband, Naomi failed to recognize this as a sign of a new season; and continued to live in Moab. Then she lost her two sons, which caused great pain and sorrow in Naomi's life. You can imagine what she might have felt in her heart. She did not even want to be called Naomi anymore.

> "But she said to them, "Do not call me Naomi; call me Mara, for the Almighty has dealt very bitterly with me. I went out full, and the LORD has brought me home again empty." (Ruth 1:20-21)

Naomi's trial was seasonal. The pain she experienced in Moab was a sign that she needed to move back to Israel. Ruth, one of her Moabite daughters-in-law, stuck by her side and returned to Israel with her. It was time for a new season in Naomi's life; and also in Ruth's life. God blessed them afterward and prospered them greatly.

We know what happened to Naomi. She became the mother-in-law of one of the richest men in Israel. If she had not gone through that trial, she would not have inherited such a great blessing. Her daughter-in-law became part of the lineage of Christ. All trials will seem painful when you are going through them, but God always brings something sweeter out of it. He is a good God.

Esther was in Persia and she was taken into the palace by the order of the king. It was a time of great pain and mental agony for Esther and her family. The enemy plotted to destroy the Jewish race from the face of the earth. In the midst of her trial, God turned her pain into great joy. She was chosen as the new Queen of Persia and greatly blessed.

Mental agony, pressure, and great stress are forerunners of spiritual breakthrough. That is the time to fast and seek God as never before. That is also the season you will least "feel" like doing any of those things. But, remember, if you want to develop your muscles you need to endure pain and show some perseverance.

The very thing you stumble over again and again in your life is the sign that you need to overcome that particular weakness or character flaw. Each of us knows what it is about ourselves that constantly irritates us. In the natural, a person receives a promotion when he does an outstanding job or does more than he is expected to do. Spiritual promotion comes the same way; when you overcome something in your character or in your heart.

Again, I am not encouraging you to pack up and move to a different location every time things are not going well in your life. Restlessness, pain, depression, dissatisfaction, etc. can also come as the result of; our own choices, an attack of the enemy, physical sickness, hormone imbalance, the result of wrong thinking, something rooted in emotionally unhealed pain from childhood, or it can be a symptom of impatience and a lack of willingness to endure right where you are.

Chapter 13

The Nations and God's Timing

"And He changes the times and the seasons;
He removes kings and raises up kings..." Daniel 2:21

"He makes nations great, and destroys them;
He enlarges nations, and guides them." Job 12:23

Each nation has a different purpose and timing on God's calendar. Each nation was created to manifest God's glory in a different way; just as each member of the body of Christ is created to manifest Christ differently. Each nation is given a specific time of glory when God's purpose is displayed through it to the rest of the world.

When we look at the ancient world, Egypt was the most blessed nation on this earth and there was a purpose for that. But, it did not last forever. Though there is a nation today with the same name, it is not the most blessed country on this earth. Most nations, when they get blessed and become number one, tend to forget God and the reason for their blessing.

God brought the people of Israel out of Egypt and gave them wealth and nations as their inheritance. Israel grew and became great on this earth. Slowly, they began to lose their focus on God and focused instead on their wealth and glory. They lost the glory and were taken as captives into foreign countries.

Then, there were the nations of Babylon, Persia, Greece, Rome, Britain, and now the United States of America. This season is for America and we do not know how long it is going to last. We are standing at the dawn of a new season and everyone is anxious to see what will happen next.

May the Lord have mercy on us and keep us strong and powerful. It is God's justice to give each nation a chance to prosper and manifest His glory through them. Each nation has a different form and style of worship and God likes them all. We need to learn to like them too and appreciate different tastes and customs.

God raises up prophets in each nation who foresee God's timing and purpose then declare it over that particular nation. This is done through preaching and proclaiming it over the airwaves. Through prophetic declaration, the destiny of that nation will begin to take shape and form. The Bible says that without prophetic utterance a nation or people perish. God said to Jeremiah the prophet, "...I ordained you a prophet to the nations." (Jeremiah 1:5)

How did God use Jeremiah to be a prophet to the nations? God put His Word in Jeremiah's mouth and told him to declare it. Whatever he spoke came to pass in each of those nations. The Bible says,

> "Then the LORD put forth his hand, and touched my mouth. And the Lord said unto me, 'Behold, I have put my words in thy mouth. See, I have this day set thee over the nations and over the kingdoms, to root out, and to pull down, and to destroy, and to throw down, to build, and to plant." (Jeremiah 1:9-10) (KJV)

The above scripture shows how prophetic declaration can affect or change a nation's destiny. As I mentioned, each nation has a specific purpose and when that season comes the prophet needs to step up to receive God's vision and declare it to the government and people. If there is no prophet or prophetic utterance, God's purpose cannot unfold.

The following scriptures make this very clear to us.

> "The instant I speak concerning a nation and concerning a kingdom, to pluck up, to pull down, and to destroy it, if that nation against whom I have spoken turns from its evil, I will relent of the disaster that I thought to bring upon it. And the instant I speak concerning a nation and concerning a kingdom, to build and to plant it, if it does evil in My sight so that it does not obey My voice, then I will relent concerning the good with which I said I would benefit it." (Jeremiah 18:7-10)

We see in the book of Samuel how God used him to shape the destiny of Israel. At the end of the book of Judges the Bible says, "In those days there was no king in Israel; everyone did what was right in his own eyes." (Judges 21:25)

Wow! That is a very scary situation. During his time the priesthood was corrupted. Though God raised up judges; their spiritual influence did not last long.

> "Wherefore the sin of the young men was very great before the Lord: for men abhorred the offering of the LORD." (1 Samuel 2:17) (KJV)

The priests slept with the women who assembled at the door of the tabernacle and brought great shame to the Lord and his name.

> "Now Eli was very old, and heard all that his sons did unto all Israel; and how they lay with the women that assembled at the door of the tabernacle of the congregation." (1 Samuel 2:22) (KJV)

What was the reason for such an apostate season in Israel's history? I believe it occurred because there was no prophetic utterance until the time of Samuel. Though there might have been prophets, there was no one whom God raised up as a national voice for Himself. The Bible says,

> "And the word of the LORD was rare in those days; there was no widespread revelation." (1 Samuel 3:1)

God raised Samuel up to be His prophet and whatever he said came to pass. The Bible says, "The Lord was with Samuel as he grew up; he did not let any of Samuel's messages fail to come true." (1 Samuel 3:19) (NCV)

God also spoke to Samuel concerning the house of Eli and the future of the nation of Israel, all of which came to pass (1 Samuel 3:11-18). God used Samuel to take Israel into the new season of being ruled by kings. This new season was not just the desire of the people. I believe it was the plan of God because God spoke repeatedly to Abraham, Isaac and Jacob that kings would come from them (Genesis 17:6; 17:16; 35:11). So, at some point, God planned for Israel to be ruled by kings.

During the time of the kings, whenever they disobeyed or rebelled against God He sent a prophet to utter judgment and restoration to them. Half of the Bible is written by prophets and contains prophetic utterances.

I believe that in every season God will raise up prophetic voices who will utter His purpose over each nation. The Bible says God will do nothing unless He tells the prophets His secrets (Amos 3:7).

We read in the prophetic books of the Old Testament specific prophecies spoken over individual nations. If we study their history, we find that all of the prophecies concerning those nations were fulfilled.

> "The word of the LORD which came to Jeremiah the prophet against the nations. Against Egypt." (Jeremiah 46:1-2)

> "The word of the LORD that came to Jeremiah the prophet against the Philistines..." (Jeremiah 47:1)

> "Against Moab. Thus says the LORD of hosts, the God of Israel..." (Jeremiah 48:1)

There are many other references in the Bible. Jeremiah 49:1; 50:1; 51:1; and Isaiah chapters 13-24 are only some of the prophetic judgments declared over nations.

Israel as God's Timepiece

The nation of Israel plays a pivotal role in world history. From the time God chose Abraham and made a covenant with him, everything else God did on this earth has been based on that covenant He made with one individual.

The covenant was not just for Abraham but his descendants after him, as well. God said that He will bless all the families of the earth through Abraham and his seed.

As we see in the Bible, Abraham's seed has not always been faithful to follow God and His commandments. Whenever they went astray He chastised them by letting them be overtaken by enemies, eventually to the point of captivity to foreign lands. God's covenant is eternal and He cannot change His Word.

Every time the nation of Israel became backslidden, God sent either a prophet or famine or attack from the enemy or civil uprising, or even led Israel away as captives to other nations. These were signs from God to tell His people that it was time to return to Him. Most of the time, Israel did not heed these warnings and, consequently, perished at the hands of their enemies.

Some Christians believe that the parable of the fig tree Jesus shared in the Gospels talks about the restoration of the nation of Israel. If we read those verses in light of the context, we will see He is not talking about the restoration of the nation of Israel. He was talking about things that are going to happen after the Tribulation.

Jesus was using a natural example to prove spiritual timing. When the leaves come out of the branches of the fig trees, it is a sign that summer is near. When all the disasters and trials that are mentioned by Jesus take place, it is a sign that the world is entering into a new season.

Please read the following verses; Matthew 24:29-35; Mark 13:24-31; Luke 21:25-33.

HISTORIC EVIDENCES

When we study the history of different nations we see how they developed through different seasons. Almost universally, the new season began with a great tragedy, crisis, war, civil war, etc. We see from the two World Wars how nations emerged as world powers as they dealt with the gruesome results of the devastation. I would like to describe precisely the history of India and the United States and show how different seasons began with unusual challenges.

INDIA

The history of India is dotted with several major milestones. India is one of the oldest civilizations on earth so there is not enough room in this book to write of every historic event (Esther 1:1; 8:9). But, I want to highlight a few that altered the national direction of India.

Let us begin with the Indus Valley Civilization around 2,500 B.C. where an urban culture was established that was based on commerce and sustained by agricultural trade. Things began to change and the country entered into a new season by the invasion of Aryan tribes migrating from the northwest into the subcontinent around 1,500 B.C.

Another major event began with the invasion of Moguls in 1,504 A.D. The Moguls were Muslims from the Middle East and they invaded India and brought a new religious concept. The Moguls brought the religion of Islam to India and forced it upon people. Thousands of people were killed and the whole nation took a new turn; a turn that remains to this day.

The next event was the colonization of India by the British and other European countries. Colonizers brought new language, customs, and industrialization to India but the people in India did not have the freedom to be in power or operate their own business. That brought the beginning of the struggle for freedom.

After a long time of struggle, India received independence from the British in 1947 and the nation entered into another new season. Since then, India has faced many challenges but has been growing economically and militarily as a major influence in the region.

USA

I have read a little bit about the history of the United States and have noticed how different events shaped its history. Pilgrims came from Europe because of religious persecution. Since then, one major event after another shaped one of the most powerful nations on earth.

The first struggle was the American Revolution (1775-1783). It was a war for the independence of the original thirteen colonies from Great Britain. Many lives were lost and the war lasted about 9 years, the result of which was the birth of a new season in American history. In 1776 America declared its independence from Britain.

There was another war between America and Britain in 1812 which is known as the Second War of Independence. The war was for trade and economic independence. This war was one of the main turning points which led to the Industrial Revolution in America (1820-1870). It made the country stronger and more powerful economically.

The Industrial Revolution was the beginning of a new season. A multitude of inventions led to a great deal of development in the areas of transportation, agriculture and communication.

Another major event was the Civil War (1861-1865) between the Northern and Southern States. More than 600,000 lives were lost in one of the most painful experiences this nation has gone through. While there were numerous causes and effects of the Civil War, I cannot delve into all of them in this book. One of the main results was Abraham Lincoln's Emancipation Proclamation, which ended slavery and brought freedom to thousands of slaves. That was the beginning of a new season for the country.

The next event was World War I (1914-1918), which caused an economic boom and prosperity. America emerged as the major creditor and financier of post-War restoration efforts in many European countries. That did not last long, though, as the Great Depression hit the country in 1929. There was a struggle to survive as more than a quarter of the US labor force was unemployed.

The Depression continued until the onset of World War II. Though America was not planning to get involved, the bombing of Pearl Harbor by the Japanese compelled America to join the war. Entrance into WWII meant an explosion of jobs and opportunities for thousands of Americans. The war marked a shift in the economy and America emerged as one of the super powers.

As a nation, America is in the middle of a transition, spiritually and economically. We are preparing to enter a new season. The decisions that the leaders make now will determine the condition of the nation in the next season. As believers we need to pray earnestly now for our leaders so that we may lead a peaceable life.

The Church (God's people) determines the future of a nation. The solutions to the problems we go through are not in the White House or in any Parliament. They are in the House of God. Where the Church goes, a nation goes. When Jesus rose from the dead He gave all power and authority to the Church, which is His body, and not to a government.

The above examples show how nations enter into new seasons that are preceded by wars and other challenging circumstances. Individual lives are not any different. Whichever nation you are from, you can look back at the history of your nation and see how different seasons began with wars, struggles, or new freedoms.

This world is going through a process of ending one season and entering another. It is happening according to God's timetable. When we observe the nations around the world, most of them are going through political and economic problems for which they do not have answers.

Nations rising up against nations, wars and rumors of wars, frequent earthquakes and calamities: though we live in the most prosperous time on earth, there are more people living in poverty and without food than at any other time in history.

Jesus said when these things happen it is the beginning of the sorrows or birth pangs of the coming of a new season.

Mark 13:8 says,

> "Nations will fight against other nations, and kingdoms against other kingdoms. There will be earthquakes in differ-

ent places, and there will be times when there is no food for people to eat. These things are like the first pains when something new is about to be born." (NCV)

The whole world is getting ready for the coming of our Lord Jesus Christ. Though we have more advanced technologies in all fields of study and greater luxuries than any other generation before us, we also have more financial problems, health issues, and moral degradation than any other generation in the past.

Whether you believe it or not, the present life on this earth is drawing to a close. Prepare to meet the Lord and live intentionally—live for what is eternal. Many nations are going through political unrest and financial crisis and people are anxious about their future. The world is getting ready for a new season politically and spiritually. It may be the prophetic sign of the one-world government under the rule of Antichrist.

Chapter 14

THE LOCAL CHURCH AND GOD'S TIMING

"...We live in an important time. It is now time for you to wake up from your sleep, because our salvation is nearer now than when we first believed."
Romans 13:11 (NCV)

EVERY LOCAL CHURCH WILL GO THROUGH DIFFERENT SEASONS IN THE SPIRIT. It is the responsibility of the leadership to discern seasons and make the necessary changes and preparations. If a church misses God's timing, that church may lose God's favor and growth. That is the reason some churches grow and some great churches die out over time.

People often think that the program and strategy they used in the last season will always work, but it will not. God will not pour out His new wine into old wineskins. You need to frequently renew and review your method of operation to see what is working and what is not working.

This is not about changing doctrines, but about changing methods. You can change your plans without changing the vision. You can change your strategy without changing your purpose. I believe the Holy Spirit has something new when we come together as a church.

If we resist the Holy Spirit and try to control Him, He will go to someplace else where He is welcome and He will be a blessing there. Those who keep up with God's timing and follow Him in every season will experience great growth and tremendous breakthroughs in their region.

Each local church is comprised of different members of the body of Christ. If a local church was started by God, it was started to manifest God's glory in a particular way in that locality. Maybe it is through worship, administration, influencing the government, prophetic words and utterances, encounters with the spiritual realm, etc. As it says in Ephesians 3:10, one of the purposes of the church is to make known to the principalities and powers the manifold wisdom of God.

If a local church is not growing, it is missing or has missed God's timing for that season. Whatever has life will keep growing. Wherever God is; there is life. You recognize life by movement, growth, and vigor. If an organism lacks these things it is considered dead.

We see around the world that those local churches that do not recognize the new season in the spirit and refuse to cooperate with Him, miss out on what God is doing today on this earth and lose their membership. All they have to say is how much greater and more wonderful things were in the old days compared to now.

God is a God of new wine, but He will not pour out that new wine into old wineskins. If He does, the Bible says the wineskin will tear apart and lose both the skin and the wine (Matthew 9:17).

Old wineskins represent rules, methods, organizations, ways, or programs and traditions that God used to accomplish His purpose in the past. If it is old and stands in the way of the Lord and quenches the moving of the Spirit, then it needs to be renewed or replaced. I believe God hates human tradition more than He hates anything else. Tradition is formed based on how God moved in the previous season and we expect Him to move and do the same within the limits of what He has done before. As you know, we cannot keep God in a box. God is not for an organized religion.

Nowhere in the Bible are we given a particular order of a church service. Every time you gather as a church and repeat the same routine or program you always had without being open to God doing something new, you have fallen victim to tradition. The Holy Spirit never does the same thing twice. He has something new to say and do every time His Church comes together to experience God.

Many incorrectly interpret the scripture which says our God is a God of order.

"For God is not the author of confusion but of peace..."

"Let all things be done decently and in order." (1 Corinthians 14:33 & 40)

As a result, they keep doing what they are used to doing and will not change. This particular scripture is not talking about the program or method we use for every meeting or the particular order of how to conduct a service. The above verse is talking about when the Holy Spirit moves fresh in each meeting through different people giving prophetic words, and the interpretation of tongues. Those things need to be done in an orderly manner. It is talking about how each individual should operate in his or her spiritual gifts when they come together as a body.

I have experienced this in different cultures so I understand this. I grew up attending a church in India that, when the congregation came together for worship on Sunday, sang two songs, then said two prayers, then had the reading of a Psalm, then testimonies, then offering and, lastly, the preaching of the Word. Year after year I sat through it and I always knew what to expect when I got to a meeting.

Each church develops its own traditions. I have watched and observed this also in different cultures. There have been numerous meetings where I have sensed the Holy Spirit wanting to move in a different direction, but those who were in leadership ignored it because they did not understand, were afraid of losing members, add were constrained by time, or afraid to step out to see what would happen if they did something different on one Sunday.

The Early Church

The Church that we see today did not exist in the Bible. What I mean is the way the church functions and the operation of ministry is far from what we read in the Bible. I am not saying everything we do is wrong, but there is some good stuff the Church left out for personal glory. The Church has experienced a lot of changes and seasons since the time it was first started. We are going to look in the book of Acts to learn of some of those changes and seasons they went through.

The Church began on the day of Pentecost with three thousand souls getting saved in one day, and in just one preaching. There was no organized program or time limit to any service. Everything depended on the Holy Spirit and what He decided to do. The following verses explain the life of the believers.

> "Now all who believed were together, and had all things in common, and sold their possessions and goods, and divided them among all, as anyone had need. So continuing daily with one accord in the temple, and breaking bread from house to house, they ate their food with gladness and simplicity of heart." (Acts 2:44-46)

> "Now the multitude of those who believed were of one heart and one soul; neither did anyone say that any of the things he possessed was his own, but they had all things in common. Nor was there anyone among them who lacked; for all who were possessors of lands or houses sold them, and brought the proceeds of the things that were sold, and laid them at the apostles' feet; and they distributed to each as anyone had need." (Acts 4:32, 34-35)

We do not see any organized worship service or fundraising for the church building in the early Church. They had services every day and they went anywhere from three to five hours (Acts 5:1-11 & 42).

The glory and power of God was so strong in the Church that it brought fear to both believers and unbelievers. There were no sick or poor in the Church. The ministry of angels was active and they helped the spreading of the gospel. Angels are not allowed to preach the gospel but they are assigned to help those who preach the gospel with power.

The first season of the Church ended when persecution arose against the believers in Jerusalem. They were all scattered throughout the regions of Judea and Samaria, except the apostles (Acts 8:1).

During Paul's apostolic ministry we do not see him teaching anyone to sell everything they had and bring it to him. But, he insisted on equality among believers. We read that in 2 Corinthians 8:13-14, "For I do not mean that others should be eased and you burdened; but by an equality, that now at this time your abundance may supply their lack, that their abundance also may supply your lack- that there may be equality."

Paul taught that each one should give as he purposed in his heart and he also said that if we give sparingly we will reap sparingly, but if we sow bountifully we will also reap bountifully (2 Corinthians 9:6-7).

THE PROBLEM WITH THE PRESENT CHURCH

Unfortunately, today many churches, as soon as they have 25 members, begin to focus on buildings and other gadgets that are needed for ministry instead of trying to meet the needs of the people and build them up in the spirit. I believe the most expensive projects most churches undertake these days are their building projects. We do not see building projects anywhere in the New Testament.

I believe Paul established churches that grew to thousands of members and they somehow managed without a multi-million dollar building project. I am not against building projects, I have done it and I might do so again in the future. I am against idolizing buildings above people and building personal kingdoms. I think it is the spirit of Babylon that infiltrates the hearts of many leaders today and there is a competition to see who owns the biggest and most expensive building.

Christianity in many European countries is fading away. Magnificent and empty Cathedrals and Christian monuments are still standing as silent witnesses of early days of glory and power. They have become tourist attractions and some of those buildings are being turned into mosques for the Islamic faith. What a sad testimony to the Gospel of Christ.

It was not because they did not have an adequate building that Christianity became irrelevant, but somewhere along the way we lost the focus of the most important mission of the Church on this earth. My prayer is that the same story will not be repeated in any other culture and that we learn from the mistakes of our past leaders.

The book of Acts says that it is impossible to reach divine unity when there is inequality and grudges in the heart of the believers. Because there is no unity, we do not often see the mighty manifestation of the Spirit in our churches. The reason there is no unity is because there is no true love.

The most we have is a good "feeling" of God's presence. We do not see in the book of Acts anyone feeling the presence of God. It says everyone in the Church was healed (Acts 4:13) and there was no lack. The apostles and believers performed mighty miracles.

God is withholding His power and glory from the present Church for our own good. If the power and glory manifested like it did in the early Church, many of us would be dead. So, God lets us experience as much as we can handle, which is just a good "feeling" most of the time. If we want more of His glory and power, then we need to cooperate with Him and walk uprightly.

Throughout the Bible we see immediate judgment whenever the glory of God was present and someone committed disobedience. Also, when those who were walking in such glory disobeyed God in any regard, they were immediately judged.

The early Church had such glory and power that if someone lied in the presence of God, they were struck dead. We see that in the book of Acts chapter 5 with Ananias and Sapphira. They sold their possessions and kept some for themselves, then lied to Peter and the Holy Spirit saying they gave it all to God. There was immediate judgment and within three hours they both were struck dead (Acts 5:1-11).

What would happen if God did the same in today's Church? I believe God wants His Church to walk in both power and obedience and is preparing a remnant to manifest and carry His glory in this end time.

We see in the Garden of Eden that the glory of God was present and covered Adam and Eve. Their disobedience brought immediate judgment and they lost the glory, felt ashamed, and lost the Garden.

Another example in the Old Testament is King Uzziah. God blessed and prospered him in everything he did, but at the end he became prideful and entered the temple to offer incense, which was supposed to be offered only by the priests. We need to know that in the Old Testament the glory or the presence of God dwelt only in the temple. Uzziah entered the temple but the priest came to stop him from doing it. The king became very angry and; before his anger had even diminished, judgment came upon him. God struck him with leprosy on his forehead and Uzziah died a leper.

> "And they withstood King Uzziah, and said to him, "It is not for you, Uzziah, to burn incense to the LORD, but for the priests, the sons of Aaron, who are consecrated to burn incense. Get out of the sanctuary, for you have trespassed! You shall have no honor from the LORD God." Then Uzziah became furious; and he had a censer in his hand to burn incense. And while he was angry with the priests, leprosy broke out on his forehead, before the priests in the house of the LORD, beside the incense altar." (2 Chronicles 26:18-19)

During the wilderness journey, God appointed Aaron as the high priest and his sons as priests to minister to the Lord in the tabernacle. It was only Aaron who was appointed to burn incense before the Lord. It was only after his death that his children were to take his place. But one day the glory of the Lord was present and two of the sons of Aaron, Nadab and Abihu, decided to bring incense before the Lord, which was not commanded them.

There was immediate judgment. Fire came down from God and consumed both of them and they died (Leviticus 10:1-2). At the end of Leviticus 9 we read that the glory of God appeared to all the people and a fire came down and consumed the burnt offering and the fat on the altar (Leviticus 9:23-24).

Today, the gospel of cheap grace has infiltrated the Church and many believers. They say, "We are not perfect so it is okay to lie once in a while and judge other people." They say, "If we commit a sin it is not necessary to ask forgiveness to the person who is offended, but just ask God to forgive you." If those people come together in a church, no glory will manifest there. No, not if we want to enter into the glory of God. No liars, or thieves, or adulterers will ever stand in His presence. God has already begun to cleanse his temples, (we are the temple), because He wants to pour His glory and power once again upon His Church.

As I write this book, God has shown me areas in my own life that need to be corrected and brought in line with the Word of God. I believe and pray that He will do the same in your life. Some are generational sins and others are my own transgressions. It is painful when God deals with our sins, but He is a loving Father and He corrects us with love and great kindness. The Bible says, "No flesh should glory in His presence." (1 Corinthians 1:29)

One of the reasons I believe the devil did not get a second chance to repent is because he knew God and was dwelling in His presence and glory. There was no excuse for him. The Bible says the devil knows God and trembles at His presence (James 2:19).

If we look into many local churches they are not running any differently than a local business or country club. Many are profit-motivated and income-based. I believe before Jesus comes the Church will go back to its original roots of love, unity, and power. It is time for a change.

Salvation is a free gift and our God is a forgiving and merciful God. At the same time, He is not a sugar daddy or a Santa Claus as some seem to think. Many say it does not matter, whatever you do He loves you. That is true but we need to know that every action has a consequence and whatever we sow we will also reap on this earth.

It is our responsibility to keep ourselves pure, holy, and useful for the Master. The Bible says, "But in a great house there are not only vessels of gold and silver, but also of wood and clay, some for honor and some for dishonor. Therefore **if anyone cleanses himself** from the latter, he will be a vessel for honor, sanctified and useful for the Master, prepared for every good work." (2 Timothy 2:20-21) (Emphasis added)

> "For this is the will of God, your sanctification: that you should abstain from sexual immorality; that each of you should know how to possess his own vessel in sanctification and honor, not in passion of lust, like the Gentiles who do not know God." (1 Thessalonians 4:3-5)

In the New Testament we read about God judging people for their sins, especially for sexual sins (Colossians 3:5-6; 1 Thessalonians 4:4-6; Hebrews 13:4). Jesus said that for every idle word we speak, we will have to give an account on the day of judgment (Matthew 12:36-37). The Gospel of Matthew, chapters five to seven, contains the new moral and spiritual standard every believer needs to abide by.

Do not be deceived by the watered down gospel of some. The New Testament depicts God as love—which is true—but that is only one side of His nature. At the same time, He is depicted as a consuming fire (1 John 4:16; Hebrews 12:29).

God can communicate His timing concerning a local church by using any one of the means I have mentioned in this book. It is the responsibility of the leadership to seek God and sense His timing when it arrives.

Chapter 15

CHANGE AND GOD'S TIMING

"Because they do not change,
Therefore they do not fear God."
Psalm 55:19b

IN EACH SEASON OF YOUR LIFE, CHANGE IS INEVITABLE. In fact, entering into a new season is all about change. If you are not willing to change, forget about entering into a new season. Every season requires a change in our **attitude, mindsets and habits**. Each season requires a renewing of the mind and an embracing of new principles and truths from the Word of God, which you either did not know before or thought were not for you.

David was a shepherd boy and was promoted to be a king. You cannot have the mindset of a shepherd boy and be a good king at the same time.

So, he was taken into the palace of King Saul to learn the new attitude and mindset of a king. Many try to enter into new seasons of their lives with old mindsets and their lives get shattered or broken. Imagine a king trying to rule a country with the mindset of a shepherd boy! What could be more chaotic than that?

The Bible says there are four things the earth cannot bear. Proverbs 30:21-22 states, "For three things the earth is perturbed, yes, for four it cannot bear up: For a servant when he reigns, a fool when he is filled with food..."

One translation of verse 21 says, "...when a pauper becomes a king." This speaks of one's mindset. One must be trained to think as a king or his mind will only function the way it has been programmed. Kings have a different way of thinking. A good king will only be satisfied with the best because he will be driven by a standard of excellence.

Having been around rich people from time to time, I have found that the difference between them and someone who is poor is their way of thinking. I have not found a poor person yet who is excellent in what he does, or diligent to take care of his or her possessions neatly and orderly. If they do it, it is only a matter of time before their situation will change. The Bible says in Proverbs 22:29, "Do you see a man who excels in his work? He will stand before kings; he will not stand before unknown men."

One of the main reasons most of the Israelites did not enter the Promised Land was their mindset. Though their bodies were freed from slavery they had the mind of a slave, or a grasshopper mentality. It destroyed them in the wilderness. The same thing can happen to us even though we are saved. If we do not train our minds to think the way God thinks about us, our mindsets will destroy us before we fulfill our destinies. It is not easy to change a mindset. As someone said, "You cannot teach an old dog new tricks." It takes the grace of God, the power of the Holy Spirit, and deliberate thinking to change old mindsets.

I grew up in a very legalistic Pentecostal background. Religious strongholds were fortified in my mind and I would have given my life for them. But I was indoctrinated with beliefs that were based on the wrong interpretation of Bible verses and not based on the total revelation of God's

Word. That is the way the devil attacks many Christians. He will take a line of scripture from here and there and make people believe that it is the full revelation. They become bound to it and division enters the body of Christ and causes Christians to fight one another.

Most of the body of Christ has fallen prey to this deception of the enemy. This is one of the weapons he has been using since the time of Adam. Most of the time when the enemy comes to you, he comes with the Word of God. If you are a spiritual babe, you will think that it is God who is speaking to you and get deceived. He came to Jesus the same way, but He knew better and defeated the enemy. In a spiritual battle our weapon is the sword of the Spirit, which is the Word of God; however, many forget that the enemy also uses the sword against them.

When God moved me into a new city there were circumstances and challenges where my belief system was greatly confronted. I had to make drastic changes in what I believed and some of those changes were very painful and extremely difficult. God used my own marriage to break me free from some of those religious traditions that I was following.

You can be a local Christian or a global Christian. A local Christian is the one who believes what is happening around him is the ultimate truth and anything different anywhere else is completely out of God's will or His Word. A global Christian is the one who has a much broader perspective about people and cultures, and is always concerned about how God moves differently in different countries and places; to the extent that he does not care much about what happens locally.

The truth of the matter is this; God does not want us to be just a local or a global Christian. He wants us to be a local Christian with a global mindset. When I started in the ministry I was a local Christian without a global perspective. I had to go through trials and problems and travel to other nations to change my local perfectionism to a global perspective. Now I am a local Christian with a global perspective. Thank God.

Again, let's allow the Bible to provide an example here. When Jesus started His ministry He selected 12 men to be His disciples. They were ordinary Jewish people. They had followed the law their entire lives. Now, here comes Jesus with a new revelation of God and a new message. I believe it was difficult for them to believe everything Jesus was preaching and teaching.

They did not know that their lives were entering a new season and they would have to change everything they believed to be true. In fact, they didn't even understand most of the things Jesus taught them until after the Holy Spirit came upon them on the day of Pentecost.

They were ostracized and considered a cult by the religious leaders because they were following a new leader who was not approved by their government or by their tradition. It was a big battle in their minds and they often questioned Jesus about what they were hearing. He then had to explain it to them and break it into pieces so they could digest the truths and form a new mindset.

When He sent them out to minister, Jesus told them specifically not to go the way of the Gentiles. This is the way it was in three and a half years of ministry with Him. After the ascension of Jesus, the Holy Spirit came upon the 120 and a new dispensation started. Now it was not just for the Jews to enjoy salvation and the baptism of the Holy Spirit. It was for the Gentiles also, but the early apostles and the Church did not want to minister to the Gentiles; only to the Jews.

The disciples' three and a half years of ministry with Jesus had formed a mindset in them, which they found difficult to change. Mindsets are formed based on our first experience with a new concept. It is our responsibility to change the mindset as we enter into a new season; God won't change that for us.

The last instruction Jesus gave before His ascension was to go into all the world and preach the gospel, but they were not even willing to do that, so persecution came and the early believers were scattered from Jerusalem all over the region (Acts 8:1).

Peter received the first revelation to minister to the Gentiles, but most of the church leaders opposed the idea. They did not know that they had entered a new season and now they needed to change their mindset. Their mindset was based on the prior revelation of the Word of God, but it was not the same for that new season.

God then called another apostle, Paul, to take the message of the gospel to the Gentiles. The main opposition to Paul's ministry came not from the Gentiles, but religious Jews who opposed him and his ministry wherever he went (Acts 13:45; 14:5, 19). God approved Paul's ministry with signs and wonders and he established churches with a new mindset based on the grace of God.

The early Jewish believers had a very difficult time believing the message of the gospel. To believe that God would justify a sinner based on his faith in Christ rather than works based on Moses' law was revolutionary. Even the few who believed in Christ tried to mix both law and grace and were confused about the message Paul was preaching.

Again, it was a battle between old and new mindsets. Just because something worked for you in the former season of your life does not mean it will work for you in this season. A revelation or teaching may work for a generation but it will no longer be relevant when God decides to move in a different way. A particular mindset may even be based on the Word of God, but you must mature in the things of God and develop a greater understanding of the whole revelation, rather than having a partial revelation about a particular truth.

I can imagine how difficult it would have been for them to stop doing what the law required and totally trust in the work of the cross. Naturally thinking, it must have seemed impossible because the preaching of one person was pitted against 2000 years of tradition. Sometimes I wonder what happened to all of those early Jewish believers because we do not hear about their descendants. When you refuse to change; you ultimately stop growing and God will leave you to continue where you are. He will not force anything on you.

Just before Jesus began His ministry, John the Baptist came preaching the baptism of repentance (Mark 1:4). It was a mighty movement that was ordained by God to prepare the way for Jesus. After the death and resurrection of Jesus, what John the Baptist taught became irrelevant. After the death and resurrection of Jesus, people received remission of sins not through baptism, but by faith in Jesus and in His blood.

During his journey, Paul found some believers in Ephesus and asked if they had received baptism in the Holy Spirit. They said they had not even heard about the Holy Spirit (Acts 19:1-6). Paul baptized them again and they received the Holy Spirit. Unfortunately, even today the doctrine of John the Baptist is being taught in some parts of the body of Christ. They believe that unless a person is baptized he or she is not saved.

When the early Church was born everyone sold what they had and brought it to the apostles, who divided it among the believers according to their needs. Everyone had an equal amount of things and, when someone had a need, those who were in charge would distribute those resources so that everyone's needs were met.

I believe it was a great blessing to the believers and it was a testimony to the people outside about the love believers had for each other. Imagine teaching that to the people in today's churches. Today, many so-called apostles are getting richer and richer but most of the believers remain where they are financially.

For most people, it is not easy to change their location or mindset. They are comfortable where they are and refuse to come out of their comfort zones. I have seen these people end up getting spiritually and physically sick because they refused the move of the Holy Spirit in their lives and continued to stick with their own agendas. Dear friends, it requires great faith and courage to move into God's timing. God repeatedly told Joshua to be strong and courageous.

Sometimes we get stuck with silly concepts in our minds and we think it is impossible to do something in any other way. When I wrote my first three books, I spent a lot of time alone in a quiet place writing them and it formed a mindset in me. I believed that if I was going to write a book I needed to be alone somewhere, away from my kids and family.

Whenever other people asked me how I wrote my books, (to get help writing their books), I used to tell them they need to be alone and not bothered by anyone to get it finished properly. Now I can tell you that is not true because when I wrote this book I did not go to a quiet place.

I was with my family and my three children were jumping around and things were flying over my head for fourteen hours a day while I was sitting in the living room typing my book. Their noise did not bother me at all and the revelation kept coming into my spirit. That experience broke my mindset and now I know I can write books at any place and at any time as long as I am connected to the Holy Spirit.

Another mindset I had about writing was that if I was going to write a book, first I needed to write the manuscript into a notebook and then type it into my computer. I did not know if I could type my book on a computer when I first wrote it, at least when I first receive the revelation because when I wrote my first books I wrote them into a notebook and then typed them into a computer.

That experience formed a mindset in me, which also was broken when I wrote this book. As I received the revelation, I typed it into my laptop. That was a big change for me, and I thank God for it. It might sound silly but that is the way mindsets are formed. Somehow we believe that something cannot be done in any other way than we did it the first time.

Mindsets are formed based on your first experience with a new concept. It could be difficult to change some of them because the more we do things in a certain way, the stronger the mindsets become. I could find scriptural reference to support my belief about writing by hand into a notebook and not using a computer or laptop, saying God told Moses to write what he heard Him speak.

But, that does not mean that what was required of one person for one event will be required by God in my life or in your life. This is the way tradition or legalism is formed. When you enter into a new season, you might need to change some of those mindsets that were formed based on your personal experiences but have nothing to do with God or the Word of God. Dare to think differently and do things differently than you used to.

Moses was born into a Jewish family and he spent some of his babyhood with his parents. Then he was taken to Pharaoh's palace to start his new season. He was there for forty years and the time came for him to enter yet another new season. He had to leave the palace and run away without knowing where he was going. Imagine that. He was living in the most luxurious place on this earth where food and everything he needed was at his fingertips, but now he had to leave all of that and live in a wilderness feeding sheep. The Bible says he ran away not because he was afraid, but because of his purpose and the call of God on his life (Hebrews 11:24-27).

You would think no one in their right mind would ever do that. Well, do you want to fulfill God's purpose for your life? Do you want to discern God's timing and move into it? You may have to take such drastic steps of faith. It may be a temporary change for a greater glory at the end. Many are called but few are chosen.

Most will not dare to take such a bold step because it would scare the life out of them. After the end of another forty years, Moses entered into another new season where he had a deeper revelation of God and intimacy with Him. Now Moses was entering into his new season where it was not him who lived but God living through Him. That is why Paul said in the Epistle to the Galatians that it was no longer he that lived but Christ living in him (Galatians 2:20). He said that because of the level of intimacy he had with Christ. He was so close to Him that he lost himself in Christ.

I have seen individuals and local churches die in their pain because they refused to change or did not know how to change. If you do not know what to do in the midst of your pain, please seek some spiritual counsel from godly men and women who are mature in the things of God. God will speak through them because they have been through what you are going through and they will have a heart to help.

Do not be afraid of change, or afraid to change. Change is necessary for growth. God loves change and those who are willing to change. Throughout the Bible we see how He interacted with people differently in each generation. Many think they need to become more religious to be blessed by God. There is only one thing you might need to be blessed and used by God and that is to be willing to change.

Chapter 16

SPIRITUAL COVERING AND GOD'S TIMING

"For even if you had ten thousand others to teach you about Christ, you have only one spiritual father. For I became your father in Christ Jesus when I preached the Good News to you." 1 Corinthians 4:15 (NLT)

A FTER I ENTERED FULL-TIME MINISTRY, I HEARD PEOPLE TALK ABOUT HAVING A SPIRITUAL COVERING, SPIRITUAL FATHER OR A MENTOR. I did not know who that person would be or how to find him. At some point, because of pride and ignorance, I began to think I did not need a spiritual covering because I thought my call was different from everyone else. Meanwhile, my life and ministry were not growing as they were supposed to and I always felt something missing.

I did not have anyone from whom I could receive counsel or ask questions. When I got into trouble I tried to handle it myself and bore the pain in my heart. Have you been there? God did not send anyone my way for 15 years and the preachers that I wanted to have as my spiritual covering were not humanly accessible. I would like to explain a little bit about spiritual covering for those who are new to this concept.

WHAT IS SPIRITUAL COVERING?

Early in my ministry, I had yet to receive proper teaching on the subject of spiritual covering. Spiritual covering means you are connected to someone whom God is using and you submit to his spiritual authority for accountability, growth and protection. There is a difference between a spiritual father and spiritual covering, or a mentor. Most of the time the person through whom you came to the Lord will be your spiritual father. Your spiritual covering or mentor is a person whom God sends your way to train you, mentor you or develop you in the things of the Spirit.

You have a personal or spiritual relationship with that person. It may be your pastor. If you are part of a larger church and you do not have a personal relationship with your pastor, God will appoint someone in that church to be your mentor. In the modern day it may be difficult to have a personal relationship with your spiritual father because people might come to the Lord through mass crusades or media. In that case, God will send someone your way to be your spiritual covering or a mentor.

1 Corinthians 4:15 says,

> "For though you might have ten thousand instructors in Christ, yet you do not have many fathers; for in Christ Jesus I have begotten you through the gospel."

Philemon 10 says,

> "I appeal to you for my son Onesimus, whom I have begotten while in my chains."

Your spiritual covering may or may not be your spiritual father. God may appoint people in different seasons for different purposes to be your spiritual covering or mentor. But, it is important to know you have only one spiritual father and may have more than one spiritual covering or mentor.

In the natural, when a child is born that child has a father and mother. Their responsibility is to nurture and care for that child. Ultimately, God is the Father of us all, but He appoints humans to show His love and care to people. When a person is born in the spirit, that person will have a spiritual father or mother. When a ministry is born, that ministry needs a spiritual father or covering. If a child or ministry does not have a father, that child or ministry is either an orphan, illegitimate or rebellious. In the ministry, the person who ordains you is your spiritual covering. There are some children who do not want to submit to their father or mother and they are in rebellion. If you are working at a company you have a boss. If you start a business you need a mentor from whom you will receive wisdom and counsel.

Why do we need a spiritual covering? An earthly father is a visible representation of the heavenly Father. One of the greatest things lacking in the world today is the father; people who are willing to take responsibility for their children. There are men who will produce offspring but are not willing to fulfill the role of a father. Similarly, one of the greatest things lacking in the Kingdom is the spiritual father. A father is someone who trains and disciplines us and from whom we glean wisdom and knowledge about life on this earth. Their heart is to nurture, protect and care for us so we will grow and become everything God wants us to be.

If you are in full-time ministry you do not run around looking for a spiritual covering. God will bring that person to your life and when you meet him both of you will know it in the spirit. It is not just one person knowing and asking the other person to do something he does not want to do. It is a principle that is mentioned throughout the Bible. Moses had his father-in-law as his mentor or spiritual covering. Elisha had Elijah. Timothy had Paul and Paul had Ananias first, and then Barnabas, and then later the church at Antioch as his covering.

None of these people went around looking for a spiritual covering. God brought it to them at the right time. I believe Elijah had someone in his early life as his mentor. Samuel started the prophetic school before Elijah and Elijah may have been trained in that school. Later in life, Elijah did not have anyone to go to when he was disappointed. David had Samuel as his spiritual covering. Depending on the different seasons and areas of your life, God can use different people to be your mentor or spiritual covering. Some may be for financial covering and others for ministry or spiritual purposes.

If you are a believer, God will raise up or send a minister to your region and He will lead you to that person or church in His time. Whatever God does on this earth, He does through His people. Whomever God uses on this earth He anoints. There are different kinds of anointing though it is the same Holy Spirit (1 Corinthians14:4, 11). When God anoints a person he receives spiritual influence or jurisdiction over certain areas and localities. Whoever comes in contact with that person comes under the influence of that anointing. When that person travels, he carries that influence with him. It is like coming into an arc of a power source.

You respect and love your spiritual covering in a godly way. It is not spiritual control in any sense though there are people who abuse their spiritual authority to control other individuals; which is witchcraft. As believers, we are supposed to be led first and foremost by the Holy Spirit.

Every believer needs to be under the influence of some anointing in order to prosper. Every minister needs a spiritual covering and those who are called into a five-fold ministry office need to submit to someone who is also functioning in a five-fold ministry capacity. As Paul said, "Submitting to one another in the fear of God." (Ephesians 5:21)

The Church is called the body of Christ. A body is made up of many members, each member with a different function. One part of the body cannot function fully on its own. Each part needs to be connected to other parts and then joined to the head, which controls and directs the function.

Romans 12:4-5 says,

> "For as we have many members in one body, but all the members do not have the same function, so we, being many, are one body in Christ, and individually members of one another."

The reason the Church is not manifesting the fullness of Christ is because many members think they can function independently of the others. They form little groups here and there and try to manifest the whole Christ. It will never happen. Christ will be made manifest to this earth when each member of the body of Christ (the Church) is knitted and joined together with the others and working together.

Ephesians 4:15b-16 says,

> "May grow up in all things into Him who is the head—Christ —from whom the whole body, joined and knit together by what every joint supplies, according to the effective working by which every part does its share, causes growth of the body for the edifying of itself in love."

Ephesians 3:16-19 says,

> " That He would grant you, according to the riches of His glory, to be strengthened with might through His Spirit in the inner man, that Christ may dwell in your hearts through faith; that you, being rooted and grounded in love, may be able to comprehend with all the saints what is the width and length and depth and height—to know the love of Christ which passes knowledge; that you may be filled with all the **fullness of God.**" (Emphasis added)

Paul compares the Church with a human body (1 Corinthians 12:27). If a part of our body needs to function, then groups of muscles and bones need to work in unity and submission to each other. God has placed each part where it belongs for the proper functioning of the whole body. That is the same with the body of Christ. Jesus has appointed each member with the needed ability to the proper place.

Each member of the body needs to work in unity and submission to others. No one is exempt from being under authority. Jesus worked under the authority of His Father (John 5:19). The Holy Spirit works under authority (John 16:13-14). How much more should we function under authority and submission who are empowered by the Holy Spirit?

WHO QUALIFIES TO BE
YOUR SPIRITUAL COVERING?

Every believer needs to be under the spiritual covering of a local church and a pastor. Secondly, that person has to be anointed and functioning in one of the five-fold ministry gifts. God has priests and kings on this earth (Ex.19:6; 1 Peter 2:9; Rev.1:6). The priests today are those in full-time ministry. Kings are business owners or those working for a business, and those in governmental positions. Every king needs a priest to act as a spiritual covering and priests need a king, or kings, to provide for them.

In the Old Testament the priest appointed kings, but the kings did not appoint priests. The kings facilitate and provide for the priests to minister to God and to the people. Priests are appointed by God just as the five-fold ministry gifts are appointed by God. No one self-appoints or appoints someone else to the five-fold ministry. In the Kingdom, the anointing flows through spiritual authority. God works through authority and anyone who rebels against God's appointed authority can bring God's judgment upon them (Romans 13:1-2).

In the New Testament Church, every believer is a priest and a king (1 Peter 2:9; Revelation 1:6). But, each of us will have our primary and secondary functions. I have seen believers who are called into the business world struggle in their life because they did not have proper spiritual covering. They might be a member of a local church and have a pastor, but they may not be submitted to them as their spiritual covering. I have seen businesses fail to prosper and even crumble because they do not come under the proper spiritual covering. If you are a businessman and are under the spiritual covering of a man of God, make sure you bless him financially as God prospers your business.

I have also seen ministers and pastors struggle and fail for lack of spiritual covering. No one is exempt and no one receives a 'Super calling' that exempts him from being accountable to another person. If you are not experiencing growth in either business or ministry, check your spiritual covering.

BENEFITS OF SPIRITUAL COVERING

The number one benefit of being under God-ordained covering is spiritual and physical protection. The best example is the story of Abraham and Lot in the Old Testament. Lot started out with Abraham and prospered in everything as long as he was with Abraham. Then there was strife between their servants and they both separated from each other (Genesis 13:7-13).

Lot moved out of his spiritual covering and opened his life to the enemy's attack. He settled in Sodom and Gomorrah and enemies came and captured both he and his family (Genesis 14:11-12). Abraham had to rescue him and his substance. The rest of the story about Lot is totally chaotic and his two daughters produced two races from him called the Moabites and the Ammonites, which were cursed (Genesis 19:36-37).

The next benefit of having spiritual covering is spiritual and financial prosperity. If you have spiritual covering, it increases your spiritual influence and positions you for financial prosperity. The story of the disciples is the best example of this principle.

One day Jesus was teaching by the Lake of Gennesaret. He had to use Simon's (who later became Peter) boat to teach the multitude because they were thronging to hear the Word of God. After He taught the people, Jesus asked Simon to put the net down into the deep for a catch. Simon replied and said they were toiling all night and could not catch anything, but he obeyed His voice and caught so many fish that the net was almost broken. They had to call their partners to help them collect the fish, causing both of their boats to almost sink (Luke 5:1-11).

I believe this happened because the disciples listened to the voice of Jesus. The moment they obeyed His voice, they stepped into the arc of His anointing. That means they came under His spiritual covering, and the anointing that was upon Jesus brought those fish into their net. How do I know that? It says in the Bible that after the miracle, Simon was so convicted of his sin that he fell at Jesus' feet.

That means the Holy Spirit touched his heart and brought revelation into his spirit about who Jesus was (Luke 5:8). That is what happens when you have proper spiritual covering. Whatever you are trying to make happen in your life and however you may be struggling to prosper, when you come under proper spiritual covering and listen to the voice of God that comes from that covering, things will happen in an accelerated mode.

I did not know where I would find my spiritual covering and I wanted the right person whom God had appointed. We were living in Denver, Colorado and I was traveling back and forth to India and to other places. I met many pastors and ministers in the US but God did not confirm them to me or me to them, to be my spiritual covering.

Beginning in September of 2006 and lasting for several months, my wife and I went through the most painful season of our lives. Never before had I experienced pain like that. I thought I was finished with ministry and should go to a secular job. All hope was lost and I thought I was not even called into the ministry anymore. It was a trial beyond description.

My wife and I had been praying and talking about what we should do next. We felt that we should go and serve another ministry for a while and wait on God. We kept praying and the names of a few different ministers were on our hearts. We decided to go to Europe to work with a ministry that does the same kind of work we do in India because we were burned out by doing ministry by ourselves. We also knew we needed more training, and spiritual covering.

After communicating and making the necessary connections, we were invited to go and serve as volunteers for a new church that was being planted. My wife and I traveled overseas to attend the first service of the new church. I felt strongly that I needed to be there for the opening of the church and we also wanted to spy out the land to know how to prepare as we were planning to relocate there for a season.

It was a difficult trip because there was much tension between us. In fact, it was the most painful trip we have ever had. We were so irritated at each other and I was so offended. We did not even have one single peaceful conversation that entire trip. But, God was doing something powerful in the unseen.

That was the beginning of a new season in our life. We went in obedience to His leading. The first church service took place on a Saturday morning and we were seated in the first row with some special guests. Guess who was sitting next to me? It was the pastor whom I had been waiting to meet all my life. I was seated right next to him!

As soon as we met each other something sparked in both of our spirits. Later that weekend it was made clear that we both felt that this was a divine appointment. Two weeks after returning to Denver, I traveled to spend time with him and visit his church. It was one of the most blessed times that I have ever had in my life. I had the best time ministering at his wonderful church. It was during this trip that I asked him if he would consider being my pastor and spiritual covering. He agreed. God used him and his ministry to bring healing and restoration to my life, family, and ministry. Thank God.

Chapter 17

YOUR FAITH AND GOD'S TIMING

"For in it the righteousness of God is revealed
from faith to faith; as it is written,
"The just shall live by faith." Romans 1:17

IT IS VERY IMPORTANT TO UNDERSTAND FAITH WHEN YOU WANT TO MOVE IN GOD'S TIMING. Without faith it is impossible to please God. Without faith it is impossible to follow God's timing. Faith is required when you do anything *with* God or anything He *tells* you to do. The Bible says that whatever does not originate in faith is sin (Romans 14:23).

If the ministry or work you are doing does not require any faith, then it is not His ministry or work. You are doing something in your own strength and it is an abomination to Him. Know this, that whenever God asks you to do something it will seem humanly impossible. This is because He wants you to depend on Him; not because He is so needy of your dependency, but because He wants us to be in partnership with Him in everything He does on this earth. The earth and its fullness belong to Him (Psalm 24:1).

Let me tell you an important truth. There are two major areas where many people make mistakes in their lives when it comes to God's timing. They are in the areas of faith and falling prey to the enemy's deception. I have seen people called by God to do great things when they were teenagers or in their early twenties, who did not obey the call because they did not know how to prepare or how faith works. Instead, they trusted in their own understanding and either failed or delayed God's plan for their lives for many years. Later, when they are in their forties or even sixties, they try to do what they were supposed to do when they were in their twenties. As I said earlier, if you miss one season, God will give you another season, but the time you spent you will never get back.

This happens to people because of a lack of understanding of the Word of God, or because there was no one to mentor them in the things of God when they were spiritually growing up. When Abraham was called by God and was given a bunch of promises, there was not one piece of physical evidence or material blessing, or any sign from heaven to assure him of those words. You might say that it was God who gave him those promises and that was enough. Then, how come we cannot believe most of the things the Bible says?

I believe Abraham had the same struggle with his flesh that we have, but he took a step of faith based on what he heard and obeyed God. Every time you enter into a new season with God, a new level of faith is required. Without faith you will never move into a new season with God.

As I was growing up, I thought this faith walk would get easier after I practiced it for a while. Let me tell you it does not. Every season requires a higher level of faith, but each time you can be sure that everything will work out for your good because you have tasted that God is faithful to His Word and you can trust what He says. It is time for you to develop your faith muscles so that you can make a higher leap of faith.

You keep growing in God each time you use that faith muscle. God always starts with the low point and raises the bar each time. In the beginning of my ministry I had to use my faith to believe God for ten rupees (20 cents). Now, I do not need to use my faith for ten rupees because I am in a different season in my life and my needs are different. Now I need to believe for one million rupees per month and I need to use all of my faith muscles to believe for it.

When we started our ministry we had only a 10 watt sound system, which we used to tie behind a bicycle and preach around the town. Now we have a 20,000 watt sound system and it took a higher level of faith to receive that. For Christians, walking by faith is not an option but a commandment (Hebrews 10:38). Without faith it is impossible to please God (Hebrews 11:6).

WHAT IS FAITH?

There are different levels and kinds of faith. Faith simply believes that you have something, or that something you are praying for and desiring has happened before you see it with your natural eyes, and acting as if it is done. Faith is not a feeling and it is not an emotion. Faith is an invisible substance by which God created the entire universe. The words of your mouth determine the level of your faith. Faith comes from God. If you have not heard from Him, the feeling you have about something is not faith, it is just presumption.

Faith always comes by hearing the Word of God. Faith is created by the Word of God. Faith is an invisible and spiritual substance created in us when we hear the Word of God being preached or we hear it from God Himself. Faith is a spirit that proceeds from God (2 Corinthians 4:13). Without the Word there is no faith, and without faith the Word will not work. When we speak the Word of God the same invisible substance is being released to accomplish what we prayed or spoke.

Every human being operates in a certain amount of faith. What differentiates the faith of a Christian from the faith of an unbeliever is the *object* of faith. In every instance, faith comes by hearing or through knowledge. For instance, if you are flying in an airplane to a particular place, you had faith in that airplane to carry you through the air to that destination. If you did not have faith, you would not have started your journey. You heard or read about that airplane and you booked your ticket based on what you knew. Then you prepared for that journey.

You did not see that airplane before you purchased your ticket and you did not see your seat, but you believed that it was going to be there. That is natural faith. The same principle applies when you want to receive something from God by faith. When you hear the Word of God, you are prompted to take certain actions in order to reach certain destinations spiritually; and you believe that it is going to happen for you before it actually does.

Faith vs. Presumption

It is very important to know the difference between faith and presumption. Faith always comes by hearing the *rhema* or spoken Word of God. If you have not heard from God, then you have no basis for stepping out in faith. Presumption comes through assumption and feelings. Just because Peter walked on the water does not mean that you can go and walk on the water whenever you want. If you feel that way, it is presumption.

Presumption is when you base your faith on someone else's experience and expect the same thing to happen in your life that happened to them. Presumption is expecting God to show up where He has not promised. Presumption is building your faith based on your past experience. Presumption is acting out what you feel, assuming it is faith.

You cannot take a step of faith until you hear from God. Many people make mistakes here and I have done the same many times. I said, "The Bible says this...," or, "I heard the preacher saying this or that." No. Just because something is written in the Bible does not mean it is for your specific purpose. Until God inspires it and gives it to you for that particular time and season, do not make a move.

Also, know that when God speaks something He will be very specific. Our God is a God of specific and detailed instruction. If he asks you to build an ark, He will tell you what kind of wood you should use and what size the ark should be. It is very important to pay attention to the specific instructions of God for you to succeed in life.

If you are not sure and the task is so great, it is fine to ask God to confirm it more than once. In that situation He usually uses other people and circumstances to show you His specific plan. He did that to Paul when He called him into the ministry. At the encounter at Damascus Paul asked the Lord what he must do. Jesus told him to go into the city and he would be told what he must do (Acts 9:6). The Lord used another disciple called Ananias to communicate His purpose to him (Acts 9:15-16).

If He says, "I have given you a house," do not go and sign a mortgage to buy a house, because He did not tell you to do that. He said He is going to *give* you a house. It is like when you need a car and you have been looking for one for a long time. One day you meet your wealthy friend and he says, "I am going to give you a new car." Will you go and buy a car then? No, you will wait for him to give you the new car.

God works the same way. If He tells you to go to a place, do not start a church or a business there because He did not tell you that. He just said to go. Many people say, "I stepped out in faith and I failed," or "God did not show up." He will not show up where He has not promised to show up. You step out in faith only after you hear the specific instruction from Him.

Peter's example in the gospel helps us understand the difference between faith and presumption. Peter was in the boat with the other disciples and Jesus came walking on the water. When Peter saw Jesus, he asked if he could walk on the water and come to Him. Jesus told him to come. Then Peter stepped out in faith and began to walk toward Jesus.

If Jesus had not told Peter to come, he would have had no business stepping out in *faith*. Do not do it or you will fail. I heard someone saying, "Whatever is God-inspired He will prepare and whatever is man-inspired he will perspire." Always know that faith comes by hearing. If you have not heard from God, there is no faith. It is either feeling or presumption.

Just because you obey God's voice does not mean that you are always in for a pleasant experience. Most of the time it will not make any sense to the natural mind why we are doing what we are doing. But, in the end, everything will make sense. You will never be a loser if you do the will of God. Maybe for a while it might seem like you are losing, but once you are sure you are doing the right thing it is just a matter of time and God will restore everything, even more than you asked or imagined.

Each time we read about faith in the Bible and how people did extraordinary things, we see it was always based on God's spoken Word. The woman with the issue of blood went and touched the hem of Jesus' garment and received her healing. The Bible says she heard about Jesus and pressed through the crowd. She had faith and her faith came by hearing about Jesus. That is why Jesus told her that her faith had made her whole (Mark 5:34).

I have learned in my life not to step out and do things until I hear from God. During their wilderness journey, the Israelites went out to fight against their enemies without hearing from God. They were defeated and their enemies discomfited them (Numbers 14:39-45). God is not responsible for our mistakes. We need to take responsibility for them. Is there a way we can learn to walk in faith? Yes. I want to share with you how you can learn to walk in faith for the rest of your life.

FOUNDATIONS OF WALKING IN FAITH

The Bible says in 2 Corinthians 5:7, "For we walk by faith, not by sight."

Anyone can walk by faith. The Bible says the just shall live by faith (Romans 1:17; Galatians 3:11; Hebrews 10:38). God expects us to walk by faith. If this were not possible, He would not require it of us. If we know the principles that are laid out in the Bible and practice them, anyone can walk by faith. You do not have to be super human or a spiritual giant to do this. It is possible for every believer and it is required of every believer to live by faith. As the Bible says, without faith it is impossible to please God. Then, we should know how to walk in faith that works all the time.

There is no such thing as faith that works sometimes, but not at other times. People say that because of ignorance of the Word of God. The faith that you received from God will work all the time and you will have it all the time. Faith will not leave you and come back after a break. I want to share with you from the Word how to have victorious faith all the time.

When God calls us to do something significant there are five foundations upon which our faith must be based. One of the reasons many attempts fail is because people do not follow these foundational principles before they begin a venture.

1) HEAR THE VOICE OF GOD

When God wants to do something significant in or through your life, He will communicate that with you in a way that you properly understand. Unless you hear from God clearly, do not step out to do anything. Many times we get in trouble because we misinterpret what God speaks to us. When God speaks a word, do not make a sentence out of it; and when He speaks a sentence do not make it a paragraph. Do exactly what He says, how He says it. You need to follow these principles only when you have a specific assignment from the Lord to do something significant. You do not need to wait for God to speak before you believe and act on practical principles such as; salvation, healing, prosperity, etc., that are applicable to every believer.

As I shared previously, faith always comes by hearing the Word of God. How do you hear God's voice? You hear God's voice when you spend time with Him in worship and meditate on His Word. There is a difference between hearing the Word of God and hearing the voice of God.

When you read the Word of God or when you hear it preached, the Holy Spirit highlights certain portions of what you read and hear. He will speak to your spirit so that you are hearing the voice of God. This can happen at any time. He can inspire the Word that is in your heart and bring something from your spirit to your memory.

The Bible says in Deuteronomy 28:1,

> "Now it shall come to pass, if you diligently obey the voice of the LORD your God, to observe carefully all His commandments which I command you today, that the LORD your God will set you high above all nations of the earth."

Exodus 15:26 says,

> "And [God] said, "If you diligently heed the voice of the

LORD your God and do what is right in His sight, give ear to His commandments and keep all His statutes, I will put none of the diseases on you which I have brought on the Egyptians. For I am the LORD who heals you."

These two verses, and many others in the Bible, specifically talk about hearing the voice of God. Jesus said, "My sheep hear My voice" (John 10:27). Any child of God can hear from Him and if you are a child of God, you *must* hear the voice of God. The Bible says, "For as many as are led by the Spirit of God, these are sons of God." (Romans 8:14)

If you do not hear the voice of God, check and see if you have yielded your life fully to Him. There are two reasons you do not hear the voice of God; either you do not know how to recognize His voice, or you are walking in rebellion.

The voice of the Lord is something you hear daily, either apart from or when you read the Bible. The voice of the Lord is when you hear from God directions or solutions to the questions or problems you face in your life. It could be a verse or word already written in the Bible, or it could be a fresh revelation, but His counsel will never contradict the written Word of God. When you hear the voice of the LORD, faith is created in your heart and spirit. You believe that voice and take action according to the direction of the Holy Spirit.

If you have not heard from Him, there is no faith. As I mentioned earlier in this chapter, just because it is written in the Word of God does not mean that it will work for your given situation. God must inspire it and speak to your spirit through His Holy Spirit.

The best example is when Jesus was tempted by the devil in the wilderness. Luke 4:1 says Jesus was filled with the Holy Spirit, and then the Spirit led Him to the wilderness to be tempted by the devil. At the end of forty days the devil came and tempted Jesus, but He spoke the Word of God and defeated him.

The Holy Spirit gave those scriptures to Jesus and He spoke them as He was led by the Spirit. Jesus was led by the Spirit to go to the wilderness and He was led by the Holy Spirit the entire time He was there. When

Jesus came out of the wilderness, He came out with the power of the Holy Spirit (Luke 4:14). When you are led by the Spirit of God, you are led by the Word of God.

Let us see from the Bible how great men and women received faith in their lives. As the Bible says, "Faith comes by hearing, and hearing by the word of God" (Romans 10:17). Hebrews chapter 11 is the hall of fame for people of faith. There we see how they received faith and did mighty things by faith.

If we study this chapter in detail we see they all heard from God before they did something for Him. Though we do not see the evidence for Abel and Enoch hearing from God, we can be sure that God will not contradict His Word.

Hebrews 11:7 says,

> "By faith Noah, being divinely warned of things not yet seen..."

God spoke to Noah about the imminent destruction of the known world and asked him to prepare an ark for himself and his family, and the creatures of the earth.

Faith believes what God says before you see it with your natural eyes. We need to understand that faith is the evidence of things not *seen*, but not the evidence of things not *heard*.

Hebrews 11:8 says, "By faith Abraham obeyed when he was called to go out to the place which he would receive as an inheritance." He heard the call of God before he started the journey.

2) ASK GOD FOR HIS TIMING

After you hear the voice of God you need to discern the timing for the fulfillment of that word. That means you need to hear from God about *when* you need to take action based on that word. Certain times require immediate action but other times require you to wait years before you take any action. Wait on God or ask Him about the timing of that word.

One of the ways the devil destroys many lives is by pushing believers to act on God's promises before the time has come. Or, he tries to put fear in them to get them to delay acting when it is actually time to act. I explain in detail how the enemy works in our lives regarding God's timing in chapters nine and ten.

God promised Abraham and Sarah a child and they waited for years, but nothing seemed to happen. Though they received the promise, they did not have the revelation about God's timing for the fulfillment of that promise. So, they stepped out of God's timing and brought forth an illegitimate child. Just because God has spoken does not mean the word is for now. Until you hear "now" from God, never step out to do anything.

Many have stepped out in faith (it was actually presumption) without knowing God's timing for their lives, and brought forth a lot of damage to themselves and others. Do not start a business, ministry, or any other endeavor until you hear a "now" word from God. You might wonder then why God promises people years before He is planning to fulfill that promise. The reason is that He wants them to prepare for the fulfillment of that promise. We are always looking forward to the fulfillment. To God the preparation is as important as the fulfillment.

The greater the purpose; the earlier God tells us about it. It takes longer to prepare for certain purposes. When we study the scriptures we see it took several years before God fulfilled His promises to many of His servants. It took 25 years for Abraham, 13 years for Joseph, 13 years for David to become king and 7 more years before he became king of the whole nation of Israel. It was 14 years for Paul. They all had to wait patiently for God's timing.

What should you do after you know the time when God is planning to fulfill the promise? That is the next foundation for victorious faith.

3) ASK GOD FOR SPECIFIC DETAILS

After you receive the word and know it is time to act, you ask God for details on how to do it. Sometimes the details arrive with the word, or while you wait for the timing of God. God spoke to Noah to build an ark to save his family and the animals of the earth. He gave him specific directions about the ark; the kind of wood to be used, and even the measurements.

Now it was Noah's job to sit down and draw a blueprint and write a business plan. I do not believe Noah knew everything involved in building an ark. He might have asked other people to help him fulfill that mission.

Let us see how Noah put his faith into practice. Hebrews 11:7 says, "By faith Noah, being divinely warned..." Noah did not have to figure things out. God gave twelve specific instructions to him regarding the building of the ark. God is a God of details and specific instructions.

- The ark had to be of gopher wood (Genesis 6:14)

- It should have separate rooms (Genesis 6:14)

- Cover it inside and outside with pitch (Genesis 6:14)

- Its length should be three hundred cubits (Genesis 6:15)

- The width should be fifty cubits (Genesis 6:15)

- The height should be thirty cubits (Genesis 6:15)

- It should have a built-in window (Genesis 6:16)

- It should have a door in its side (Genesis 6:16)

- It should have three separate decks (Genesis 6:16)

- Noah should take his wife, his sons, and his son's wives (Genesis 6:18)

- Noah should take two of every animal species, male and female (Genesis 6:19-20)

- He was to take provisions; food for his family and the animals (Genesis 6:21)

Noah had to obey the instructions given by God without seeing any evidence of rain in the natural. Genesis 6:22 says, "Thus Noah did; according to all that God commanded him, so he did." Genesis 7:5 says, "And Noah did according to all that the Lord commanded him." That is true faith.

We see again in the book of Exodus that when God wanted Moses to build the tabernacle He called him up to the mountain and gave him in meticulous detail, the blueprints. Almost half of the book of Exodus, the entire book of Leviticus, and parts of the book of Numbers are dedicated to the details of building the tabernacle, and its services.

It amazes me how many details God gave in those books about the tabernacle. I believe this is because He knows that we will mess it up if we do not have the details. Each believer is being built by the Holy Spirit to be a living temple of God to offer spiritual sacrifices (Ephesians 2:20-22; 1 Peter 2:5). Whatever He wants us to do; we need to receive the detailed plan from Him.

Similarly, David had a desire to build a temple for the Lord. God spoke to him and said it was not David but his son, Solomon, who should build the temple. David acquired the gold, silver, and other precious materials to build the temple. He charged his son and made him the new King of Israel. It took seven years and 183,300 people to complete the building project (1 Kings 5:13-16; 6:38).

When Jesus sent His disciples out to minister He gave them specific instructions of what they must and must not do. In Matthew 10 we read more than 38 specific instructions He gave to them. In Luke 10, when He sent out the seventy to preach the gospel, He also gave them specific details.

Sometimes, until we do our part, God will not move and do His part. We see that in the life of Jesus when He fed the five thousand. He asked the disciples to arrange the crowd to sit in rows of fifty. I believe it took more than two hours to arrange such a crowd in rows of fifty. There were five thousand men and many more women and children. Until the disciples did their part, Jesus did not perform any miracle. It took planning and organization to arrange the crowd. The Bible says in Proverbs 15:22, "Plans fail for lack of counsel, but with many advisers they succeed." (NIV)

4) PREPARE A DETAILED PLAN

After we receive the specific directions from God it is time for us to act. It is time for us to put our brains to work. We need to make a plan to collect the needed materials and put on paper the entire project and its timeline. As you make plans, seek wise counsel and glean from other godly people about how they did certain things.

Many fail because they neglect this part. They do not plan wisely how to execute what God has spoken. They wait for God to do everything when it is time to take action. The Bible says, "Plans are established by counsel…" (Proverbs 20:18). As someone said, "If you fail to plan; you are planning to fail."

Jesus said when we plan to build a tower we need to make sure we have all the money and strength to finish the task. In Luke 14:28-32 we read, "For which of you, intending to build a tower, does not sit down first and count the cost, whether he has enough to finish it—lest, after he has laid the foundation, and is not able to finish, all who see it begin to mock him, saying, "This man began to build and was not able to finish. Or, what king, going to make war against another king, does not sit down first and consider whether he is able with ten thousand to meet him who comes against him with twenty thousand? Or else, while the other is still a great way off, he sends a delegation and asks conditions of peace."

In the above scriptures, Jesus is using a natural principle to explain a spiritual truth. After you receive the word it is time to act. You need to sit down and prepare a plan to accomplish the task. Sometimes this happens during the time between when you hear the voice of God and when you wait for the timing of God. This is the time we need to put our brain to work. We need people whom God has anointed with the spirit of wisdom in that specific area.

Asking wise counsel from other people does not mean we do not trust God. Some people are so "super spiritual" they have no clue how things work in the natural. These people do not accomplish much in and with their lives.

Exodus 31:1-5 says, "Then the Lord spoke to Moses, saying: "See, I have called by name Bezalel the son of Uri, the son of Hur, of the tribe of Judah. And I have filled him with the Spirit of God, in wisdom, in understanding, in knowledge, and in all manner of workmanship, to design artistic works, to work in gold, in silver, in bronze, in cutting jewels for setting, in carving wood, and to work in all manner of workmanship."

I believe all God's great purposes include a business side to them. Whenever money is involved to accomplish any of God's purposes, there has to be a business plan. You need people with experience in business and money to give you counsel and direction about executing that plan. Sometimes you will need engineers, bank managers, accountants, lawyers, artists, musicians, computer designers, or architects, etc. to accomplish what God has spoken to you.

5) Discover Your Level of Faith

When God trains us in the area of faith, He trains us in different levels. Much like natural education, you start at the nursery level and advance to whichever level you want to study. Everyone must start with the nursery. Similarly, exercising our faith graduates us to different levels. We see an interesting pattern in the Gospels of how Jesus trained His disciples in the area of faith. They started out with no faith, then they had little faith, then they had the mustard seed faith, then they grew into the last level of faith which is mountain moving faith, or great faith.

Mark 4:40 says,

> "But He said to them, "Why are you so fearful? How is it that you have *no faith*?""

Mark 9:19 says,

> "He answered him and said, "O *faithless* generation, how long shall I be with you? How long shall I bear with you? Bring him to Me.""

In the above scriptures Jesus is talking about His disciples. The first was when they were on the sea. The storm came and they all became fearful. Jesus rebuked the storm and calmed the sea, and then told the disciples they could do the same if they had faith. The next scripture is when a father brought his demon-possessed son to the disciples to cast the demon out but they could not. Jesus said the demon did not leave because they did not have any faith.

The disciples went from having *no faith* to *little faith* in their next season of training with Jesus.

Matthew 16:8 says,

"But Jesus, being aware of it, said to them, "O you of *little faith*, why do you reason among yourselves because you have brought no bread?"

Matthew 14:31 says,

"And immediately Jesus stretched out His hand and caught him, and said to him, "O you of *little faith*, why did you doubt?"

I am using the type of wording that is mentioned in the different incidents in the Gospels, not necessarily in the chronological order of these events. Different authors of the Gospels use different wording for the same incidents. But, I believe the Holy Spirit guided the authors to reveal certain truths to us though they use different words to explain the same incidents.

Then, we see in the Gospels the disciples asking Jesus to increase their faith. You can only increase what you already have. He shared with them the mustard seed principle of faith.

Luke 17:5-6 says,

"And the apostles said to the Lord, "Increase our faith."

So the Lord said, "If you have faith as a mustard seed, you can say to this mulberry tree, 'Be pulled up by the roots and be planted in the sea,' and it would obey you."

I am particularly choosing what Luke said in his Gospel to explain this principle. Matthew said that if you have faith as a mustard seed you can say to this mountain (Matthew 17:20). Luke says that if you have faith as a mustard seed you will say to this mulberry tree, 'Be pulled up by the roots and be planted in the sea, 'and it would obey you.'

The disciples went from having no faith to little faith, to mustard seed faith or mulberry tree moving faith, and then we see Jesus talking to them about mountain moving faith.

Matthew 21:21-22 says,

"So Jesus answered and said to them, "Assuredly, I say to you, if you have faith and do not doubt, you will not only do what was done to the fig tree, but also if you say to this mountain, 'Be removed and be cast into the sea,' it will be done. And whatever things you ask in prayer, believing, you will receive."

Jesus said this right after he cursed the fig tree and it was dried up from the root. Now He is talking to the disciples about the real faith that moves mountains. It is also called *great faith* in the Gospels. Matthew 8:10 says, "When Jesus heard it, He marveled, and said to those who followed, "Assuredly, I say to you, I have not found **such great faith**, not even in Israel!" (Emphasis added).

A person can receive mountain moving faith as a gift from the Holy Spirit, which is called the gift of faith. When you have this faith, nothing is impossible to you. That is why Jesus said all things are possible to those who believe (Mark 9:23). The good news for us as believers is that we do not need to start with having no faith. God has given each born-again believer a measure of faith according to Romans 12:3. It says, "For I say, through the grace given to me, to everyone who is among you, not to think of himself more highly than he ought to think, but to think soberly, as God has dealt to each one a measure of faith."

Each believer has received a measure of faith from God. It is up to us whether to increase that faith or not. As I mentioned earlier, you can increase only what you already have. Like everything else in the Kingdom, the more we exercise the faith God has given us the more it will grow.

We grow in our faith to different levels. First of all, we need to determine which level we are at. To find out which level we are at, we need to see what we are able to believe God for without being stressed out. Acting on the faith that God has given you is as normal as breathing. If you are struggling with your faith about what you are believing God for, then what you are believing does not match your level. Find someone who is at that level and ask them to believe with you. Two are better than one.

Exercising your faith is like exercising your body. We each have a level of how high we can jump. If you try to jump higher than you are able now, you are asking for trouble. That does not mean you will never be able to jump higher than you do now. Of course you can, but you have not practiced enough. The more you keep jumping, the higher and better you will jump.

This is also true with an exercise machine. If you go to a gym to exercise you need to start with a level your body can handle. If you never lifted any weight before but try to lift 200 pounds, I am sure you will get crushed. The same principle applies in the spirit.

Faith works the same way. You start with the level at which you are able to believe God and when you receive that your faith increases to the next level. The reason some people do not receive what they are believing God for is because they are trying to reach for a level at which they have not practiced. They jump and they fall, then they jump and they hit the bar and then they get hurt and blame God for letting them down. No, God has not let you down. You have not reached that level yet.

It is like trying to teach 10th grade math to a 4th grade student. Their understanding is not developed enough to grasp the 10th grade math. Believers often try to believe for things based on someone else's experience. They hear that someone else received something from God and all of a sudden they think they can believe and receive the same from Him. Maybe not. You do not know the whole story about their life and how they reached the point where they were able to believe God for what they received. Just because my friend can do the 10th grade math does not mean I can do it if I am only in 4th grade. I need to grow in my understanding of math by going from one level to the next until I reach the 10th grade. It takes time.

How do you know if you are trying to believe for something that is not on your level? You doubt, you sweat, you shiver, you are not sure sometimes, then you are sure other times. Your faith will be like the electricity in India; it always fluctuates high and low. That is not faith. That is called being doubtful or double minded. Faith is like a rock; once you get it, it cannot be shaken or moved. Can you remember an incident like that in your life? A time when you first prayed or believed and just knew in your heart that you had what you were believing for?

When I started in the ministry we walked door to door distributing gospel tracts. Then, we thought it would be nice if we could rent a bicycle and go to preach, but we did not have any money. It took only one rupee, which was only two cents in American currency, to rent the bike for an hour. We had to believe God to receive two cents to rent a bicycle. God met that need and our faith increased to the next level. Because we had to rent the bike by the hour we had a desire to own a bicycle so that we did not need to worry about how long we were gone to preach the gospel.

We believed God and He opened the door and gave us a bicycle. What if I said, "I received the bicycle and now I want an airplane, so let's believe for it?" That would have been foolishness! It is not that God was not able to give me an airplane. Of course He could. But, I did not know anything about airplanes. I had never even flown in an airplane before. I did not know how to take care of one.

When we received our bicycle, our faith increased and grew to the next level. The mustard seed principle was at work here. When you plant one mustard seed you receive innumerable mustard seeds and then you plant them again to go to the next level. So, we decided to believe God for a motorcycle. It was a big leap of faith. We knew in our hearts God had given it to us. After a while the motorcycle came. Our faith grew again to the next level.

We began to believe God for a three wheeler (it is a type of taxi in India). God gave it to one of our friends and we went to preach the gospel in that three wheeler. Then we believed God for a car, then for vans, and then for buses. We have had a few buses so far in our ministry; right now we have two. It is not a big thing to believe God for a bus. Though we do not have the money with us right now, we have the faith. Faith is the substance of things hoped for, the evidence of things not seen. I do not need to believe now for a bicycle, I am already past that level. Like when you are in 10th grade, the 1st grade math is not a challenge.

God in His infinite wisdom deals with us as we deal with our children. He will not require of us faith that we do not have. When He asks us to do something, He knows that we have the faith to believe it and do it. Before He asks you to pray for the healing of someone's cancer, He will train you to overcome your own headaches by faith. He trains us and takes us from one level to the next, but from experience I can tell you He requires the maximum and the best of what we have.

So, before you step out to do something significant for God or for yourself, make sure you follow these guidelines. They will keep you from a lot of trouble and unnecessary pain. Faith is seeing what you need in your life in the invisible realm. You can see in your heart that it does exist and it is real, but it is in the form of invisible substance. Now it needs to manifest in the visible realm. Speaking it out transforms the invisible substance into visible substance. Thanking God for it positions you to receive it, praising God for it releases it.

FAITH AND WORKS

This chapter would not be complete unless I talk about works. Christians are called the people of faith. Most people believe God is great and capable of doing great things. That does not mean their faith is benefiting them in any way. To many, their level of faith never goes beyond the stage of feeling to the level of action. Real faith always prompts us to take corresponding action. The Bible says faith without works is dead (James 2:14-26). Faith and work always go hand in hand just like the two rails on a train track. Works without faith is performance or religion.

James 2:17 says,

> "In the same way, faith that is alone—that does nothing—is dead." (NCV)

The Greek word for work used in the Bible is *ergon* which means;

1. Do business, employment, that with which anyone is occupied; 2. Any product whatever, anything accomplished by hand, art, industry, mind; 3. An act, deed, thing done (from Thayer's Greek Lexicon).

When we go from one season to the next in our lives, God will require us to do something we never did before. Sometimes the action we take is the catalyst for the beginning of a new season. Many wait around for God to do what they are supposed to do and never make any progress in their Christian life.

Once we have followed the above guidelines and know it is God's time to act, we need to step out in faith. That does not mean there is no risk involved. Every time we obey God there is risk involved. If there is no risk it is not of faith. Noah had never seen rain in his life, but he prepared the ark at the voice of God. There was a tremendous amount of risk involved in building a humongous ark.

Without faith it is impossible to please God. Without risk it is impossible to act in faith. The only difference is that when you take a risk in order to act in faith; there will be no fear in your heart. You will be fully assured that God will back up your actions and fulfill His Word that He promised. He is always faithful to His Word. Faith is made perfect by what we do in faith.

James 2:22 says,

> "So you see that Abraham's faith and the things he did worked together. His faith was made perfect by what he did." (NCV)

Chapter 18

RECOGNIZING YOUR *KAIROS* MOMENT

"For an angel went down at a certain time into the pool and stirred up the water; then whoever stepped in first, after the stirring of the water, was made well of whatever disease he had." John 5:4

THE GREEK WORD *KAIROS* IS USED TO DESCRIBE A MOMENT OR PARTICULAR SEASON IN TIME, RELATED TO OUR LIFE ON THIS EARTH. A *kairos* moment is when God intervenes in our circumstances and opens a window of opportunity in the spirit or in the natural, prompting us to take a step of faith. Most of the time, the *kairos* moment comes in the midst of a crisis.

Our response to His prompting will determine whether or not we will enter into our next season. In the spirit it can happen when you pray, worship, or in a corporate meeting where God moves upon our spirit to obey His voice. I have missed God in some of those moments in my life. He was gracious enough to give me a second chance.

In the natural it can happen with a divine appointment, or suddenly you are faced with an opportunity to make progress in your purpose. Please know that it takes faith to please God and step into your *kairos* moment.

As we have seen with the lame man at the pool of Bethesda, or the widow during Elijah's time, they stepped into their *kairos* moment and received their miracle. A miracle occurs each time you step into a *kairos* moment in the spirit. Your deliverance, healing, and financial breakthrough all depend on recognizing this moment, stepping out in faith and receiving it.

Walking in the spirit means learning to recognize the *kairos* moments and walk in them. One of the secrets of the success in Jesus' ministry was that His actions were dictated by His recognition of the *kairos* moments.

The first miracle Jesus did to manifest His glory is the best example for this. The family who was hosting the party was suddenly faced with a crisis. They did not have enough wine for the guests. They told His mother and she told Jesus. Jesus replied and said His time had not yet come.

That means the *kairos* moment for Him to move in their circumstance and meet that particular need had not yet come. When the *kairos* moment came, He told the people to fill the jars with water. Their obedience to His voice determined the outcome of their crisis.

They recognized the *kairos* moment and filled the jars with water, then the miracle took place. If we learn to recognize the *kairos* moment, every crisis we face is an opportunity for God to manifest His glory. Amen.

I believe we are in a time of restoration. There are many in the body of Christ who missed their *kairos* moments and are living in disappointment. These are people who once walked with God and were passionate for His Kingdom but are not walking with Him now. There are many who were wounded on the battlefield and are walking around with their wounds, not knowing what to do. These are wounds of disappointment, betrayal, rejection, failure, and sin.

Jesus is coming back for a victorious Church. He has begun a season of restoration. It includes the restoration of the five-fold ministry gifts, the ministry of the saints, and comforting those who mourn in Zion to give them a garment of praise instead of the heart of heaviness.

The enemy has made many believe that their case is irreparable and they have to live the rest of their lives with their mess and the regrets of unwise decisions. I want to tell you that is not true. There is not a situation where Jesus cannot restore someone. I want you to be encouraged and speak hope into your hopeless situations. God says in Jeremiah 30:17, "For I will restore health to you and heal you of your wounds."

Our God is a God of compassion and kindness; full of mercy. Some of you might be thinking about your lost seasons and how you missed your *kairos* moments. As I shared earlier in this book, if you have missed one season in life you will get another season. In the natural we have the same seasons year after year.

That is why the Bible says, "To everything there is a season, a time for every purpose under heaven" Ecclesiastes 3:1. Though you can never get back time once you spend it, you will get another season; another opportunity to make the right choices. There are powerful examples in the New Testament about how God gives us another chance and season in life.

Many of the mistakes God's people make occur because they step out to do the right thing at the wrong time. They heard from God concerning the task they are supposed to accomplish but they did not wait for His timing. Many are in a big mess and they do not know how to get out of it.

Our God is a God of redemption, and He will help us to redeem whatever we have lost. It may not be easy, but it is possible. Do not look for any quick fixes. If the problem you are in right now is the result of many years of wrong choices, it may take you a few years to repair the situation and get back on track. It all depends on the circumstances.

God may not do a supernatural miracle to get us out of such situations. He wants to make sure we learned what we were supposed to learn so that we will not repeat it again because it cost us so much. Whatever we wrought with our own hands we need to work out with our human efforts.

We see a relevant incident in the book of Acts. After his conversion experience, Jesus told Paul to go into the city and there he would be told what he must do. When his sight was restored and he received physical strength, the Bible says Paul immediately began to preach.

Jesus did not ask Paul to preach. The result was the Jews plotting to kill him. Jesus did not send an angel to deliver him supernaturally. The disciples put him in a basket and lowered him from the wall of the city. Here is the greatest apostle of Jesus in a big 'basket,' (Acts 9:6-23), just like Jonah was in the belly of the great fish. That is what happens if we are not patient to wait for God's timing. We will end up in uncomfortable places that are not easy to get out of.

I believe Paul learned a lesson that day not to do anything unless he was directed by the Lord. You and I may have similar experiences in our lives. Do not wait for the supernatural to happen. Make plans and strategies to get out of the mess as soon as you can.

When Jesus began His public ministry he called twelve disciples to be with Him and sent them out to preach the gospel. He selected twelve disciples and, out of the twelve, three were very close to Him. He called three of them together in one day from the same environment and trade. They were Peter, James, and John, and they were fishermen and partners in business (Luke 5:10).

One day Jesus was teaching by the Lake of Gennesaret. The multitudes were thronging and pressed Him to hear the Word. He had to get into a boat to be safe and He asked Simon (who was later called Peter) if He could use his boat. Simon let Him use his boat. After Jesus finished teaching He told Simon to let the net down for a catch. Simon told Him that they had been trying all night to catch fish but they did not get any.

That was the beginning of a new season in Simon's life. He may have been discouraged because he did not catch anything to sell, and if he did not sell, he would not make any money. During that long night, Peter probably was not thinking that the next morning his life would change forever because he would be called by Jesus to be one of His disciples. His life was about to change for good in the midst of that disappointment.

He obeyed Jesus' word, cast his net and hauled in a miraculous catch. He could not put all the fish into his boat because there were so many, so he called his partners (James and John) to come and help. They filled both of their boats, and they began to sink. This experience touched Peter's heart. He was convicted of his sin and fell on Jesus' knees and cried for mercy. Jesus said to Simon, "Do not be afraid. From now on you will catch men." They brought their boats to the shore and they left everything and followed Jesus (Luke 5:1-11).

The three of them became Jesus' disciples that day and walked with Jesus for the next three and a half years. They were closest to Jesus among His twelve disciples. They became His very close friends and they saw many of the miracles Jesus performed. Jesus took them onto the Mount of Transfiguration and allowed them to see His glory, majesty, and power. He took them when He raised the dead. These three disciples were His inner circle and were privileged above others.

During His earthly ministry, Jesus entrusted them with, and invested in them, every part of His life so they could continue His ministry after He left. If they failed, Jesus would fail in His mission. He called them to be the pillars of the Christian faith and the Church. They did not know the full scope of their calling during those three and a half years. They thought Jesus was going to be with them physically for the rest of their lives.

When Jesus said that He was going to be crucified, they tried to talk Him out of it and were very disappointed. When Jesus was arrested by the Roman soldiers His disciples left him and ran for their lives. Peter even denied Him three times and cursed Him (Mark 14:71). When Jesus was crucified they lost all hope and thought there was no more ministry left for them.

They did not know what to do. One day Peter, James, John, and two other disciples were together and Peter said he was going fishing. The other disciples also joined him. I believe they decided to go back to their old trade in order to make a living. They did not know that God had not left them or that He was working and defeating the kingdom of darkness for them behind the scenes.

Though His disciples forsook Jesus, He kept His commitment and still went to the cross and paid for their (and our) sins. When we are not faithful, He is still faithful and concerned about our lives. He will never leave us nor forsake us.

> "Simon Peter said to them, "I am going fishing." They said to him, "We are going with you also." They went out and immediately got into the boat, and that night they caught nothing." (John 21:3)

They did not catch anything the whole night. In the morning Jesus came and stood on the shore, though they did not recognize Him (John 21:4). He asked them whether they had anything to eat.

Jesus might have felt so much pain in His heart by seeing that these precious men, with whom He entrusted His mission on this earth, had gone back to fishing; forgetting everything they had experienced, seen and heard from Him for three and a half years. They forgot all the miracles they experienced and the love He had shown them. As my pastor says, "When people lose the vision for their future, they always go back to their past."

People lose the vision for their future because of failures and disappointments in their lives. This is when they begin to accept the lie that the mistake they made is bigger than God and His mercy. It is interesting to see that before Peter ever denied Him, Jesus knew that he was going to go through a sifting by the enemy and He had already prayed for Him (Luke 22:31-32). God foreknows every challenge and temptation you and I are ever going to face and He prays and prepares a way out for us. We can be assured that Jesus' prayers shall get answered.

1 Corinthians 10:13 says,

> "No temptation has overtaken you except such as is common to man; but God is faithful, who will not allow you to be tempted beyond what you are able, but with the temptation will also make the way of escape, that you may be able to bear it."

Jesus didn't only pray for Peter and his restoration. He is seated at the right hand of God and is praying for you and me. Romans 8:34 says, "Who is he who condemns? It is Christ who died, and furthermore is also risen, who is even at the right hand of God, who also makes intercession for us."

Jesus remembered how He called them three and a half years ago. This was a similar incident and He was using this to remind them of where they came from. Jesus called them children. John 21:5 reads, "Then Jesus said to them, "Children, have you any food?" Though they forsook Him and did not believe Him, He did not scold or get angry at them. He still loved them and treated them as His children.

It was the beginning of another new season in these disciples' lives. God was working behind them and for them even though they did not have any hope for the future. I want to share with you that when you feel that all hope is lost and there is nothing left for you on this earth, know that God is working for your benefit behind the scenes, though you may not see it.

He has a plan for your life and He is not finished with you yet. You may have denied Him and let Him down. He is not angry at you nor has He forgotten you. He will come back to you and remind you of the same place He had called you from. He will give you a second chance. Please believe that each missed chance has a second chance.

You may have sinned against Him horribly and feel that you are not worthy to be forgiven. I can tell you that no one has sinned like these disciples. No one has ever forsaken Jesus like His disciples did. I say this because you and I did not get the chance to walk with Him for three and a half years.

We have not yet seen the miracles the disciples saw. We have not seen Him in person (if you have, praise God) as the disciples did. Yet, they forsook and denied Him. Still, Jesus came back to them and wanted to restore them. He wants to do the same with you or anyone you know.

Jesus told them to cast the net on the right side of the boat and they caught a large number of fish. This incident reminded John about the first miracle they had when Jesus called them.

> "Therefore that disciple whom Jesus loved said to Peter, "It is the Lord!" Now when Simon Peter heard that it was the Lord, he put on his outer garment (for he had removed it),

and plunged into the sea." (John 21:7)

They came to the shore and saw that breakfast had been readied for them. Jesus took the bread and fish and gave it to them and they had breakfast together (John 21:13). Jesus restored them, especially Peter, and loved them though they had failed Him. One of the most powerful verses in John chapter 21 is verse 14. It says,

> "This is now the third time Jesus showed Himself to His disciples after He was raised from the dead."

That means Jesus appeared to them twice before and still they did not follow Him. They were not restored in their faith; such was the pain in their heart. They might have also felt betrayed by Jesus and were offended.

God used the same Peter on the day of Pentecost when he preached the first message and three thousand people were saved. He and John healed a lame man who was lame from his mother's womb. Peter raised a girl who was dead, and his shadow healed the sick people.

> "So that they brought the sick out into the streets and laid them on beds and couches, that at least the shadow of Peter passing by might fall on some of them. Also, a multitude gathered from the surrounding cities to Jerusalem, bringing sick people and those who were tormented by unclean spirits, and they were all healed." (Acts 5:15-16)

Jesus came to them again and again until they were totally restored. I believe He would have appeared to them not two or three times but as many times as were needed to restore them. This is our Jesus. He will come to you. It does not matter how many times you might have failed Him. Or, you may have felt He has left you or betrayed you. No, He will not. He is still the same Jesus and if He came to His disciples, He will come to you. There is a new season on your horizon and He will come to you with loving arms, so wake up and be encouraged. As the Bible says,

> "Therefore strengthen the hands which hang down, and the feeble knees, and make straight paths for your feet, so that what is lame may not be dislocated, but rather be healed." (Hebrews 12:12-13)

Many of His precious saints have walked away from the call and the position He has appointed for them. Many are walking with a wounded heart, thinking that their mistake is too big to be forgiven. Others think they are living a life that is not worthy to be restored again.

You might say that Peter only messed up once but I have betrayed Jesus several times. I believe Jesus would have restored Peter regardless of how many times he betrayed Him. As long as Peter was willing to be restored, Jesus would have done it.

Jesus said that if our brother trespasses against us seven times we are commanded to forgive him or her. Not just seven times but seventy times seven.

Matthew 18:21-22 says,

> "Then Peter came to Him and said, "Lord, how often shall my brother sin against me, and I forgive him? Up to seven times?" Jesus said to him, "I do not say to you, up to seven times, but up to seventy times seven.""

Jesus practices what He preaches. If you come to Him today, He will forgive you and restore you to your purpose and calling. God bless you.

HOW CAN YOU KNOW IF YOUR TIME HAS COME?

By now you might be asking in your heart, "How can I know when my time finally comes to fulfill God's purpose for my life?" Having a strong desire in your heart is not enough to step out to do what you feel is the right thing to do.

Sometimes those desires and passions have to die before God can do anything through us. God does not want us to run depending on our energy and strength, but to run in the power of His Spirit.

Many people have desires to do something *for* God. The truth of the matter is He does not want anyone to do anything *for* Him. He is not in any need as we think of need. He said in Psalm 50:9-12, "I have no need of a bull from your stall or of goats from your pens, for every animal of the forest is mine, and the cattle on a thousand hills. I know every bird in the mountains, and the creatures of the field are mine. If I were hungry I would not tell you, for the world is mine, and all that is in it." (NIV)

Colossians 1:16 says,

> "For by Him all things were created that are in heaven and that are on earth, visible and invisible, whether thrones or dominions or principalities or powers. All things were created through Him and for Him."

Instead of trying to do things *for* God, God wants to accomplish His purpose *through* us. To do that everything that stands in His way must give way. Sometimes the very vision God gave us can stand in His way if we are trying to make it happen by our own effort and strength instead of letting Him do it through us.

We need to surrender all to Him. That phrase is a cliché in the Christian world, but only a few understand its real meaning. Many say with their mouths, "I surrender all," then go out and continue to live the same way they used to.

There are areas of our heart that are not yet surrendered to God and He alone knows them. If you ever feel that you have surrendered everything to God, beware, surrendering to do God's will is not a one-time event but a daily choice.

You need other people and circumstances to be ready for you to fulfill God's purpose. It does not happen by your power, education, or effort, but it will happen by His Spirit. That is why the Bible says in Zechariah 4:6, "...Not by might nor by power, but by My Spirit,' says the Lord of hosts."

When it is time for you to fulfill your purpose, everything you have been looking for in order to fulfill that purpose will fall in place. Relationships, resources, anointing, and open doors will all come looking for you. You do not need to go out seeking them or to create them; they will come looking for you. I am not saying that you should sit at home doing nothing and they will come to you. You need to walk daily in obedience to the voice of the Holy Spirit.

The bigger the purpose, the longer and more intense the preparation. Sometimes God has to put in place the right government and leaders to fulfill His purpose through a person. Other times, He has already formed nations and kingdoms with the right people for you to fulfill His purpose. We see that in the lives of Joseph, Moses, Jesus, Nehemiah, Esther, Daniel, etc. These people's purposes depended upon the people who were in authority during those days.

There are ministries, ministers, businesses, individuals, governments, cities, and nations that have to come into place to help you fulfill your purpose. You cannot do it alone.

Finally, you will feel a release in your spirit when the right time comes. You will have the peace of God in your heart no matter what the circumstances. May the Lord help us to fulfill all that He has for us and be found faithful when He comes. Amen.

If you were blessed by reading this book we would like to hear from you. If you would like to know more about Pastor Abraham John and the ministry or to order other books by him, or if you would like to invite him to minister, please visit www.maximpact.org

Or, write to us at:

Maximum Impact Ministries
P.O. Box 3128
Syracuse, NY 13220 USA

In India:

Maximum Impact Ministries
P.O. Box 6
Kottarakara, Kerala, 691506
India